Careers and Opportunities in the Theatre

Careers and Opportunities in the Theatre

by Jean Dalrymple

General Director

City Center Light Opera Company

City Center Drama Company

E. P. Dutton & Co., Inc.
New York 1969

Published simultaneously in Canada by
Clarke, Irwin & Company Limited, Toronto and Vancouver

Library of Congress Catalog Card Number: 68-12467

SBN 0-525-07636-0

A lifetime of work in the theatre as actress, playwright, manager, producer, press agent, and director has given me the temerity to write this book. The path of my career has wound in and out, crossed and recrossed the lives of hundreds, even thousands of others equally intent on much the same goals. To all of them, I owe an immense debt of gratitude, for each one has contributed to the sum and substance of what I have tried to set forth, and to them I dedicate this book.

My special thanks for some of the detailed information must go to Beatrice C. Cole, who did research and the preparation of the manuscript, and to Jeanne F. Bernkopf, my painstaking editor.

Contents

Illustrations

Author's Foreword

It seems to me that every day there is a flood of letters or phone calls asking for "two or three minutes" of my "valuable time" to give "some advice" about work in the theatre. A sixteen-year-old schoolgirl who addressed me as Miss Dolrinkle said she had heard and read so much about me that she was sure I could tell her how to become a famous actress. "On second thought," she added, she was not sure I was the one after all, as she was interested in becoming a famous television actress. In the same mail another young lady was perfectly sure I *was* the one because she had just seen a television production of mine.

A sixteen-year-old boy wrote from a small town in the Midwest that he wanted to become a successful gag writer and he enclosed several copies of his jokes painstakingly written in a minute hand on separate and minute pieces of paper.

A man of forty-seven wrote that he felt he had wasted his entire life but had finally made up his mind to become an actor or at least make a try at it because he had just come into a small inheritance.

Manuscripts, unsolicited of course, pour in in such profusion, most of them peremptorily demanding "an immediate reading" and my "detailed criticism," that I have been forced to demand in return a contribution to City Center—which is too often forthcoming, putting me on my honor to read "full-length comedies" of nineteen pages and poetic dramas of two hundred eighty pages on the fall of the Roman Empire.

Recently many of my good and old friends have been calling me about their budding offshoots who have decided on the theatre as their lifework. Most of the time the parents firmly insist, "Don't encourage her!" One of my friends said, "I must ask you to see her or I'll have no peace, but if you give her a job, I'll never speak to you again."

But some young people with proper background and training I have encouraged and some I have given jobs. In fact, we have quite a distinguished alumni, and not all the would-be playwrights have been without hope. The jokes the young gag writer sent me were surprisingly amusing and eventually some of them were bought by a stand-up comedian who said he and others like him are always in need of material. There are a number of excellent press agents and public relations directors who served their apprenticeships with us, and several successful directors and producers, too, started with us.

So when I was asked to write this book about your career in the theatre, I decided that since I have been in and of the theatre—in and of just about every form of the performing arts —for over thirty years, it was the logical thing to do.

Part One: On Stage

1. The Legend

That beautiful moment when the houselights dim to darkness arrives. A thousand tongues and two thousand hands are suddenly, truly still. This is the magic moment—but then a spotlight plays on the curtain, and an inconspicuously dressed man steps out to announce that the leading lady is indisposed and her part will be played by Mary Smith, the understudy.

There is a groan from the disappointed audience; several leave to demand their money back. Then the curtain rises and the show goes on. Mary Smith, a trifle nervous to start (she has heard that groan from the audience), warms up as she goes along and, to everyone's surprise, she's very, very good. In fact, at intermission there is a buzz of excitement. This girl is so good many say she is better than the star, whom they've never seen in the role.

The press agent for the play smells a story and calls the papers. He is lucky enough to find one of them interested in the Cinderella story, and so there are a reporter and a photographer backstage when Mary receives a standing ovation at the final curtain call.

A film producer, who had come to the theatre that night with thoughts of buying the play, decides it is not for him, but that young Mary Smith is just the girl he has been looking for. He rushes backstage to sign her up.

Of course all of this is a dream, but it is a dream that does come true. It happened to Shirley MacLaine, for instance, and just that way. Shirley was understudying the late Carol Haney in *Pajama Game* when Carol was taken ill and Shirley stepped into her place.

Hal Wallis, the independent producer for Paramount, and Alfred Hitchcock came to see Carol Haney for one of the leading roles in their new film, *The Trouble with Harry*. When they learned Miss Haney would not appear, Hal Wallis got up to leave, but Hitchcock said he wanted to see the show anyway. So they stayed, and Shirley was given the part in *The Trouble with Harry*.

Anita Gillette, who substituted for Anna Maria Alberghetti in *Carnival*, found her photograph and story in all of the papers the next day through the shrewd maneuvering of the producer, David Merrick; he was having a running battle with Miss Alberghetti, and so took this opportunity to tell the public that he liked Miss Gillette better. Anita was embarrassed because Anna Maria was her friend. But the publicity did make Anita Gillette a "name," and she has been kept busy in important roles on Broadway ever since.

And then there is the outstanding example of the understudy-to-stardom story. Jean Arthur was the name in a comedy having the usual difficulties during its out-of-town tryout tour. When she was taken ill and could not continue, author, director, and producer were frantic. They set about trying to find another name to replace her, but none was available. Besides, with someone new they would have to close down the tour, re-rehearse, and virtually start all over again. So why not give the understudy a chance at it? The rest is solid theatre history. Judy Holliday co-starred with Paul Douglas in *Born Yesterday*, one of the greatest successes of the 1940s.

But the success came to these girls because they were ready for it. They didn't come from nowhere. The audience may never have heard of them until that moment of truth, but agents, producers, and directors had.

The understudy today is not the stage-manager's relative or the producer's friend. Sometimes the understudy is the more qualified for the role and isn't in it simply because a name was needed to raise money for the production. He may have been an actor since he was twelve and have gone to the Professional Children's School; he may have had a graduate course at the American Academy of Dramatic Arts. He probably has had small parts in summer stock, in winter stock, and finally in an off-Broadway play which lasted just long enough for him to be seen, noticed, and tucked away in the card-index mind of the director who finally gave him his chance.

The understudy does not turn into the star very often. Most of the time when the understudy goes on, it is to do a serviceable job of "keeping the curtain up," and the management is pleased because only a few refunds have to be made. When the star returns, the understudy or standby goes back to waiting, for waiting is the main job and it takes a good deal of moral fortitude.

If the show is a musical, the understudy is usually part of the ensemble; in a straight play he may have a small role.

The designation of standby is given usually to a name performer who almost was selected to originate the leading role and as second best is well paid to rehearse the part and "stand by" for an emergency. Sometimes the standby even has another job, perhaps singing in a supper club, but he is on call and his employers must give preference to the show.

It is particularly devastating for an understudy to substitute for several performances, maybe even a week or two while the star is vacationing or ill, enjoy the luxury of the star's dressing room and private dresser and the intoxicating acclaim of the audience (for the public is invariably superkind to substitutes, first being terrified that there will be a disaster, and later being overjoyed that all has gone well), and then have to move back into the chorus or small walk-on role or whatever. I have known many of them to weep when the star returned.

But of course nothing has been lost, because if they have real talent, it will show. There is so little of it and the search for it is so thorough, especially by the much-maligned agents, that it cannot stay hidden, even in a high school production in South Dakota.

Today the agents follow up, track down, and seize upon just about anyone they believe can be developed into what they unglamorously call "a property," a pinnacle achieved through hard work, intense collaborative effort, and a few lucky breaks (some of them manufactured).

Some of the "Breaks"

It has been interesting for me to talk to some of the stars who have played at City Center and to find out how they arrived. Maureen Stapleton, who starred in one of our greatest successes, Tennessee Williams' play *The Rose Tattoo* and who at this writing is starring in Neil Simon's hilarious comedy *Plaza Suite,* got her actual start in summer theatre, but began dreaming years before.

When she was about six, Miss Stapleton saw Jean Harlow in the movies. "I thought," Miss Stapleton reminisces, "that if I became an actress I'd get to look like Jean Harlow." From that time on she talked of nothing else but becoming an actress. Her family, of course, paid no attention to her and didn't believe her until she left her hometown to go to New York.

In order to live, she found work at the Hotel New Yorker operating a billing machine, and she immediately enrolled at the New School for Social Research, where Herbert Berghof was giving courses in acting.

That summer a group of about twenty-two of Mr. Berghof's students each chipped in $150, which they had saved or borrowed, in order to rent and run a summer theatre on Long Island. None of them knew very much about running a theatre, but they put on a season of plays, doing everything from building sets to sewing their own costumes. They lived in improvised dormitories, doing their own cooking and cleaning, and living a hand-to-mouth existence, but they had a season. One of the plays they did was a successful *The Playboy of the Western World*.

Miss Stapleton returned to New York in the fall and through Mr. Berghof's influence read for Guthrie McClintic who was, by a happy coincidence, producing *The Playboy of the Western World* on Broadway. She was hired as an understudy. One day one of the cast was let out of a performance to do a radio show, and Miss Stapleton played the part of Sarah.

It was a small part, but Mr. McClintic liked her in it and gave her parts in two plays he produced—the long-running *The Barretts of Wimpole Street* which starred Mr. McClintic's wife, Katharine Cornell, and *Antony and Cleopatra*.

Miss Stapleton climbed to stardom slowly, step by step. "It was hard work," she said, "and if you can do anything else, I always tell aspiring actresses, do it! I suppose if you are really determined to be an actress, nothing will stop you. But no one should go into it with illusions. Statistics tell the grim tale of the number who try, and the few who really make it, but if you're one who has made up your mind, get enough training to add confidence to your determination. I recommend a couple of seasons of summer stock as one of the ways of getting it."

But there is no fixed method of breaking into the theatre. Summer stock gave Sandy Dennis, too, experience, but it was by one of those lucky flukes—like Lana Turner's being discovered by a talent scout while drinking a Coke in Schwab's Drug Store in Hollywood—that Miss Dennis got her first job in New York.

After a summer spent with the New London (Connecticut) players, Sandy Dennis came to New York when she was nineteen. It was early fall. A few weeks after she arrived, while walking along Broadway, a man stopped her and asked her if she was an actress. "Yes," she told him. He said he was doing an off-Broadway play, Ibsen's *The Wild Duck*, and there was a part in it for a fourteen-year-old girl which he thought she could play. Would she like to audition for it?

Sandy went down to a little theatre in the village and read for the role and was engaged. The play ran for only three weeks, but through it she interested an agent who began to get her small parts. All the while she continued classes with Herbert Berghof during the days when she wasn't rehearsing or playing matinees.

When finally her big opportunity came along in *A Thousand Clowns*, she received rave notices but not much happened to further her career until her overwhelming success in *Any Wednesday*, which gave her star status.

Then a quick jump to films for the second lead to Elizabeth Taylor in *Who's Afraid of Virginia Woolf?* brought her the Oscar for best supporting actress.

Paul Ford didn't decide to become a professional actor until he was thirty-eight years old but he says, "I was always crazy about acting. At college I was in the Dartmouth Players and I availed myself of every opportunity to do a play. In my teens, I was active in the Germantown [Philadelphia] Y.M.C.A. theatre group but I had never considered being a professional actor. I worked as a salesman and just acted for fun.

"Suddenly I decided I'd had enough of business and I wanted to follow acting as a career. I started at the very beginning—making the rounds of agents, producers, and even stopping at theatres to talk to stage managers—without any luck.

"I finally took some radio auditions and got an acting assignment on radio (this was in the days when they were really doing shows).

"My first part in the theatre was in a play called *Decision* in 1944. I didn't appear until the end of the second act. It was a small part as a police captain and my job was to arrest the lead, but from then on I was 'in.' I played in a lot of different shows, some good, some bad; some closed almost immediately, some ran five to six months.

"The big break was getting into *Command Decision* which ran for fourteen months. I got good critical notices. It was a long climb up but it was worth it. My advice to young theatrical aspirants is to hang on, work hard and, if you're lucky, the breaks will come."

Although Paul says his big break was getting into *Command Decision*, the play that made him a star was *The Teahouse of the August Moon* in which his portrayal of the frustrated civilian-colonel moved the first-night audience—even the critics —to such laughter that the play almost came to a stop several times. Paul then repeated the role for the film.

Betsy von Furstenberg was "discovered" by Alfred de Liagre. He was looking for an actress to play in *Second Threshold*, by Philip Barry. (The playwright died before it was produced and Robert Sherwood worked on the play with Mr. de Liagre.)

Deli, as he is called by his friends, knew Betsy's family but had no idea she had theatrical ambitions. Betsy was scheduled to be a debutante but, instead of making her society debut, she went to Italy and acted in a film which resulted in her getting her picture on the cover of *Look* magazine. When Deli saw that photograph, he invited her to come to his office to read for him.

"He gave me the script to study and warned me it was the only copy he had, and that I was to guard it carefully," Betsy recalls. "I promptly lost it on the Fifth Avenue bus and called him up in tears. I didn't hear from him for weeks, and I was sure I had lost my big chance because of my carelessness when one day he phoned me to come in and read for him again."

Betsy had never been on the stage before, but she had the quality Deli was looking for. She was given good notices in the part and her career was launched.

Family Influence

If you come from a theatrical family, you have open sesame as far as contacts are concerned. We are very clannish people, and we enjoy welcoming the children of well-known performers. But although nepotism is rampant in our ranks, so is the feeling that the offspring must live up to the standards set by the parent. And so sometimes a famous name can be a detriment, for just too much is expected of the young aspirant. Still, it usually helps to have a theatrical heritage.

I was trying to choose among several girls for a summer production I was directing. All of the girls were lovely and rather inexperienced. I decided on the one who was the daughter of a famous actor I knew; her background was reassuring.

A number of second-generation performers have gained fame: Jack Jones, for instance, is even better known than his "Donkey Serenade" father, Allan Jones; Judy Garland's daughter, Liza Minnelli, has reached the top ranks; so have the Fondas, Jane and Peter, Nancy Sinatra, Ethel Barrymore Colt, Helen Hayes's son, James MacArthur, Candice Bergen, and others.

2. The Giant Step

If you are determined, prepared, and ready to take the plunge to come to New York, the mecca for theatre aspirants, I hope you will arrive on a beautiful sunny day in July and that you will have a place to live. It would be nice if you had a friend here to meet you, and if that friend happened to be in the theatre, it would be very nice.

July is the month when literally dozens of plays and musicals are being cast for fall production on Broadway, off Broadway, off-off Broadway, and national tours, and the directors of out-of-town resident theatres are here looking for replacements. So that is the time to be in New York. And if you are met by a friend who is in the theatre, you can be briefed about production activities.

But if you arrive alone by bus without a definite place to go and in a pouring rain, let your youth and optimism stand you in good stead.

I suggest you check your baggage and set out first to find the spot where you will sleep that night. Unless, that is, you have come with a letter of introduction to a producer or director and feel you must head to his office at once. The chances are you will find the producer you are after is in the Virgin Islands or Palm Springs celebrating the success of his play. If he hasn't a play running, he may be in the same boat you are—looking for something to do—and unable to do anything for you until his next production.

Your spirits may be dampened by this more than by the rain.

Speaking of low spirits, if you have taken a room by yourself, it may be some time before you will be able to make friends—even acquaintances—and you will discover there is no loneliness to compare with that of being all by yourself, plunked down in the middle of eight million souls all of whom seem, in your eyes, to move about with at least one close companion.

Do you have the stamina and moral fortitude for weeks or maybe months of loneliness in a strange, overpowering, maddening, even frightening metropolis like New York? I remember the case of a European opera singer who came to New York for the first time to embark on an American career. She was here three days, canceled all her engagements, and returned to Italy with the cry: "It is all too big—too fast—too much for me!"

There is a popular Horn and Hardart's restaurant near City Center with great uncurtained plate-glass windows and sometimes when I pass by and see a lonely little figure eating a sad little meal, my heart goes out to her and my impulse is to join her for a minute or two, but of course I am in the usual New York hurry, and I never do.

Places for Girls to Live

If you are planning to live in New York, you might consider one of the clubs for those with theatrical ambitions. But decide first whether you are willing to return to almost the sort of life you had in college—a dormitory living in which you will be surrounded by new people, some of whom may reject you, for there are cliques in these dwelling places just as there were during your school days.

The Rehearsal Club at 47 West 63rd Street is famous; it was the background for the play and film *Stage Door*. To be eligible to live there, girls must be studying for the theatre, be making the rounds, auditioning, be already in the theatre, or be well enough established to have an agent. They can work as clerks or typists or baby-sitters to pay their rent, but they must spend at least 50 percent of their time on the theatre. Application is by letter or in person. The girls are carefully screened for admission.

The Club accommodates forty-one girls and the cost is under thirty dollars a week. The price includes two meals a day, seven days a week. There is a rehearsal room as well as many hotel conveniences. The girls are protected: Holmes Protective Agency night watchmen are on duty from eleven at night to six in the morning.

There are denominational homes not exclusively for theatre aspirants, such as the Studio Club of the Y.W.C.A. at 210 East 77th Street. This nine-story building accommodates one hundred forty-six girls who come from all over the world and who are primarily interested in ballet and musical comedy. It has four soundproof rehearsal rooms, pianos, and also a little recital hall. The rates are from $27.50 to $32.50 a week which includes room and two meals a day, breakfast and dinner, seven days a week.

The Evangeline Residence, 123 West 13th Street, and the Parkside Evangeline Residence at 18 Gramercy Park South, under the auspices of the Salvation Army, are residence clubs for girls from eighteen to thirty-five. These are not restricted to the arts, but many young actresses live in both clubs. The rate is from $23.50 to $26.50 a week (some double and some single rooms) and includes fourteen meals a week. Applications must be made in person and there is a waiting list.

The Ten Eyck-Troughton Memorial Residence, also financed by the Salvation Army, at 145 East 39th Street is a residence club for women from thirty-five to sixty. Many of these are women who are returning to work after being widowed or because their children are grown. They are mostly professional and business women, but there is a sprinkling of actresses among them. The club accommodates three hundred thirty women and the rate is $21.70 to $26.60 a week for fourteen meals.

There is also the East End Hotel for Women at East River Drive and 78th Street. The minimum rate is $32.75, which includes fourteen meals a week.

Young Men

If you are a boy, there are the William Sloane House at 356 West 34th Street and the West Side Y.M.C.A. at 5 West 63rd Street. Rent is approximately twenty dollars a week (or a little more depending on location and size of the room). Each has a swimming pool, health club, and hotel conveniences. Meals are bought in the cafeteria. The Y on 63rd Street has an extensive program of theatrical arts and a guidance counselor who specializes in finding part-time jobs for young men studying for the theatre or making the rounds. Application for rooms in both clubs is through the residence secretary.

Where to Eat

Dining out is a bit of a problem in New York but with a little exploring you can find many spots in this city of some 23,000 restaurants where prices are low and meals delicious.

Billy Rose once said, "I lived on two packages of salted peanuts a day for several weeks when I first started. They are the cheapest and most nourishing."

You can get a nourishing and inexpensive meal at the Y.W.C.A. cafeteria on Eighth Avenue and 50th Street, for very little money. Other cafeterias and restaurants in the theatrical district offer good food at low cost.

The Swiss Inn, 355 West 46th Street, between Eighth and

Ninth avenues, offers many appetizing four-course meals for $2.00 or less.

Un Rincon Argentino (An Argentine Corner), 1626 Broadway, grills meats in Argentine style in full view of the diners and serves many hearty dishes for 99¢ each.

The Paradise Oriental Restaurant, 311 West 41st Street, across the street from the Port Authority Bus Terminal, is an attractive Greek restaurant with excellent food at very low prices.

Max's, at 30 West 47th Street, has fresh broiled trout for only $1.25. This is a Jewish restaurant where the homemade cheese cake and apple cake are excellent and very reasonable.

If you live in the Village, Rosetta's, 502 Sixth Avenue at 13th Street, has excellent Italian meals for less than $2.00. In the East Village, Leshko's, at 111 Avenue A, is a Slavic restaurant popular with the hipsters. An order of meat-filled pirogen (equivalent to the Italian ravioli) comes seven to the plate, swimming in butter, and costs 80¢.

For sea food, within hiking distance of Broadway, there is Oscar's Salt of the Sea, 1155 Third Avenue (between 67th and 68th streets). The selective diner can eat in the neighborhood of $2.00.

The Stage Delicatessen at 834 Seventh Avenue serves sandwiches that are a meal in themselves. Joe Allen's at 326 West 46th Street is another spot favored by young actors where the food is plentiful and inexpensive.

Other restaurants where you can get a good and inexpensive meal are the Brazilian Coffee Restaurant, 70 West 46th Street, the Cabana Carioca, 123 West 45th Street, the Maginas Tavern, 304 West 40th Street, and Molfetas, 307 West 47th Street.

When you want to splurge a little, there are the Carnegie Hall Tavern at 165 West 56th Street, the Russian Tea Room at 150 West 57th Street, and Pearl's Chinese restaurant at 149 West 48th Street, all catering to artists. And don't forget the Algonquin Hotel, 59 West 44th Street, Reuben's, 6 East 58th

Street, and the Sixth Avenue Delicatessen, 1371 Sixth Avenue.

No matter what people say about the high cost of living in New York, if you do have a little money or can earn some, and if you team up with one or two others, you can get along. There are still attractive low-priced apartments in well-run buildings in the unchic sections of the West Side—which by the way is a most convenient place to live if you are going to be in the theatre. Tasty, nourishing meals cost surprisingly little if one of you is a good cook and if you curb your taste for prime steaks and caviar.

Every now and then, however, make sure to have luncheon or dinner at the West Side Sardi's at 234 West 44th Street (wonderful food at extraordinarily low prices considering the fame of the place) or Downey's, 705 Eighth Avenue, where you will be seen and where you will have the opportunity of meeting other people like yourself intent on a theatre career. If you have wealthy parents coming to visit you, or if you have a beau with a fat bankroll, have them take you to the "21" Club at 21 West 52nd Street or, later at night, to P. J. Clarke's at 915 Third Avenue.

It is very important for you to get to know as many people of the theatre as possible. You will find that doors are more easily opened for you by friends, even acquaintances, of producers and directors than by your own efforts.

Are You Sure?

What made you decide you could make a career in the theatre? Watching films and/or television, or Broadway productions which have reached your city? Have you been active in school plays, or are you a graduate of a university drama course? Have you been an outstanding success with a little theatre group? Are your parents dismayed by your decision, or is it your husband or wife who disapproves?

The urgency and strength of the call of the theatre has always surprised me. For some people it is as bad as alcohol or gambling. They wreck their lives—or so it seems to their friends and families—yet they can be satisfied only if they are in some way, in any way, working in the theatre.

It is better, in my opinion, to indulge this overpowering urge while you are still young and before you have family commitments, because you may not outgrow it. There are the cases in which a devoted wife and mother leaves her home and husband to take a "vacation" in New York to make the rounds of agents' and producers' offices. If she does, by some quirk of fate, succeed in her quest, it could well be the end of her marriage, unless she has a remarkably understanding spouse. If on the other hand, she has the usual disappointment, she will return to her home to her family's rejoicing, but to her own dissatisfaction that she tried too late.

I recently met a fine-looking woman, well over fifty, who said, "My children are all married and have moved away from us. My husband says he doesn't mind if I try to get a job in the theatre. Could you help me find an agent or introduce me to some producers?"

I imagine I showed a certain lack of encouragement because she rushed on, "I do have to play character parts now, of course, but I wouldn't mind that, and I know I'd be good if I just had a chance. I have wanted this all my life and I have got to have a try at it before I die." There were tears in her eyes.

I said I would audition her myself, and I did. She was very good. She was too old for the part, but she was right. She had had talent all her life.

But then there are those without talent who seek a career in the theatre only because they have been told—perhaps first by doting grandparents—that they are beautiful or handsome and then later, "You should be on the stage." After hearing it long enough they believe it, but they will never make a real career in the theatre. Looks alone are not enough. After all, with all of the contests from Miss America and Miss Universe down to a local Miss Hoecake, just about every girl who is not downright scary-looking can be a contestant. Male beauty doesn't have as many contest opportunities but then male beauty is rarer, which is undoubtedly why the market for this "commodity" is greater.

Even for the movies, the day of the just pretty boy or pretty girl seems to be passing. Behind the lovely facade there must be something else: a lively mind, a winning personality, an elusive charm—and talent. Talent is the important factor.

But luck too plays a star role in theatre careers. If the director of *I Can Get It for You Wholesale* hadn't wanted an oddball type to play the secretary, the success of Barbra Streisand would have been delayed, although with her enormous gifts it was bound to come. And if Mike Nichols and his associates had been unwilling to take a chance on an unknown to star in *The Graduate*, Dustin Hoffman might still be making the rounds of the off-Broadway theatre from which he catapulted to world renown.

If the lucky break doesn't come for you in the first year, the second year, even the third, do you have the intestinal fortitude to stick it out, and will it still seem worth your while? Obviously, it will be easier to get along if you have a nice fat allowance from your family. Certainly, it is not a good idea to come to New York unknown and unheralded, without either enough family backing or special skill—typing is a good one— to get you through at least a full year.

Can you stand behind the counter at Macy's or Gimbels when you are between roles or while you are waiting for that first job, and keep your charm and your cool while you toady to the often demanding, hurried customer? Or perhaps wait on table and fend off the wolves who are bound to appear from behind the menus? (Today this goes for boys as well as girls!)

If you have been hailed as a leading player in your home-

Dustin Hoffman *(left)*, star of Murray Schisgal's play,
Jimmy Shine, sharing a pause with the author. *(Friedman-Abeles)*

town little theatre or in high school or university plays, will it break your heart to learn that in New York you are regarded as just another beginner and that your amateur past glories will receive no recognition at all?

Can you read two lines of dialogue or sing three bars of a song and be sent away with a curt "Thank you," time after time? Can you bear the elation of getting a part, only to be dismissed after two days of rehearsal because the actor the director wanted all along suddenly shows up?

Ego takes a terrific beating in the theatre. When you have become an established player—even a star—you will have reviews to contend with: those of the newspaper critics and television broadcasters. "Completely inadequate," "numbingly inept," "substandard even for off-off Broadway" are some of the milder epithets applied to well-known players recently.

If your reaction to any of these moments is to think, even fleetingly, of sleeping pills, the gas oven, or the black bottle, forget show business. It is not for you!

But if you have talent, and the urge to use it; if you have good health and strong nerves; money or the ability to earn it; if you have the stamina, thick skin, and the emotional stability to accept rebuffs, disappointments, and downright rudeness—then you really owe it to yourself to keep knocking at the theatre door until it opens for you.

James Earl Jones, star of *The Great White Hope,* backstage
with playwright Howard Sackler. *(Friedman-Abeles)*

3. Getting Started

After you've checked into your new home and unpacked, go to the nearest newsstand and pick up a copy of *Show Business*. It is vitally important that you read this trade paper as well as *Variety* and *Backstage* very carefully every week. They are packed with information, and you should study them as you would the Bible. Then if you are suddenly introduced to Saint Subber, you will know he is a very active producer, not a cleric.

While you're sipping your morning coffee, take a good look at all of the casting listed in *Show Business*, make yourself an itinerary and set forth for the first time to make the rounds of producers' offices. It will not be the last time, of course, but before the day is over, you will feel almost like an old pro.

If by some good fortune—you might even say by some miracle—you are just the type a producer needs, and it will probably be for an off-Broadway play, accept what is offered even if it is only a walk-on and with virtually no money. The first step in getting into the theatre either on or off Broadway is the hardest, and any foot in the door is important.

It is much more likely, however, that you will be making the rounds for some time before you are offered a part or any kind of work in the theatre.

Some producers, not many but some, have set times and days when they interview actors even though they are not casting. (I don't know why they do this unless it is to keep themselves occupied between productions.) Still, you might be just the one to make an impression, so that it is worth the effort.

When you make the rounds, you will meet other actors who are looking for work. It won't be difficult to make friends of them, for most of them are gregarious and warmhearted. From them you can learn a great deal about where to go and whom to see, as well as where to live, where to eat, and other pretty vital information. Many lasting friendships start in the outer rooms of producers' offices.

Agents

It isn't easy to get an agent, but they will find you if you have talent. The better agents see all the off-Broadway and off-off-Broadway productions, looking for new faces. If you show any promise at all, you can be sure an agent will come backstage to talk to you.

While most agents will not take on a complete unknown, there is no harm in trying to convince them. You may find yourself turned away by the receptionist (she does the screening as a rule), but if she thinks you are a type the agent happens to be looking for at just that moment, she will ask him to see you. If you get this far with her, and she asks you to wait, be sure you do! It may be a long wait and lead to nothing, but on the other hand it may be your golden opportunity. So don't leave to keep an appointment for your hairdo or even for a class. Your hairdresser will understand and so will your teacher.

Faye Dunaway had her "head in the basin" as she puts it, when her agent called her at the hairdresser's and told her Sidney Gordon needed a quick replacement for the leading role opposite Michael Rennie in *Wake Up, Darling*, a comedy Mrs. Gordon was trying out at her Falmouth Cape Cod Playhouse.

Faye didn't even wait to dry her hair, but put a scarf around it turban fashion, was at Mrs. Gordon's office in fifteen minutes, and got the part—her first important role.

I have great respect for agents. The good ones are managers in the best sense of the word. They see that their young clients go to acting classes, take voice lessons, choose flattering hair styles, learn how to audition, take off weight, put on weight, know how to make up, and, most of all, learn how to live between jobs.

They will even get you jobs—as office helpers, salespeople, baby-sitters, photographers' models, or if you are tall, really thin, and have "clothes sense," as fashion models. And they will introduce you to people who will help you in your career.

4. Auditioning

The First Audition

Your first meeting with the playwright, director, and producer may be in the producer's office, but if it's at an audition, it could be in a dingy, unattractive rehearsal hall. It is too bad theatre stages are at such a premium today that it is unlikely any but the final auditions will take place on the real stage.

An audition is cruel and terrifying to some, particularly if it is held in a rehearsal hall where you are only ten or fifteen feet away from the usually deadpan group of people who are deciding your fate, but if you have confidence, you will accept it as your opportunity and your showcase and make the most of it. Just remember that the people who are auditioning you are eager to have you do your best and are hoping you will be the one they are looking for; in a way they are as nervous as you are, for casting can decide the success or failure of a play. So walk out before them with purpose and speak up loud and clear and give your personality a chance. Don't bury your face in the script; let them see your expression and, if the part gives you the opportunity, let them see you smile.

You will have had the opportunity of glancing over your part in the script before you are called upon to read, and the director will give you his idea of how the character should be played. Only inexperienced directors and producers ever ask an actor to read a part "cold."

At best every audition is nervous-making. Stars have told

me that they have felt frozen with fright when called upon to read for a role they particularly wanted to play; so don't let nervousness get you down. Just read the part as best you can —no one expects you to give a finished performance—and have confidence in your ability.

If you are going to audition for a particular role, dress carefully and make sure that you do not appear unkempt. It is very hard to visualize you as well-dressed if you come in looking like a beatnik, but if you come in looking well-dressed, they know there is a pretty good chance they can get you up as a beatnik.

They may be looking for a "character." If you are applying for this sort of role, you have probably decided you are not a beauty, but you still have to be prepared for such comments as, "She's homely all right, but not what we're looking for." If you are not strong enough to stand up against such thoughtlessness, rudeness, indifference, or even malice (for there are sadists in the theatre as there are in every field), you may be made pretty miserable. Just remember there are more opportunities and openings for out-of-the-ordinary-looking actors than for "typical" men and women—even though beauty will always be regarded as a priceless gift.

Second Audition

If you are asked to return for a second reading, you will be given a script of the entire play to study, and you will be able to show how the character would develop in your playing of it.

Study the lines carefully and try to understand how the character thinks. If the role is well written, you will find that the words express the character and fall into a definite pattern of speech. This is not always so if it is a colorless, small part—an unimportant friend, son or daughter—and this, therefore, is the most difficult role to play with any particular distinction. In fact, for such a minor role you will probably be

Anne Kaye and Steve Skiles, the young lovers in the marathon off-Broadway musical, *The Fantasticks,* which has played over 3,500 performances. *(Friedman-Abeles)*

selected more for your appearance, manner, and quality than for any special acting ability. The more definitive and quirky the character, the easier it will be for you to "get into it" and make a showing. But whatever the part, be sure to read the whole play so that you can understand your role in it.

Years ago actors were given "sides"—small scripts containing only the lines of their part and the last few words of the line directly preceding theirs. I never could understand how it was possible for any actor to know what he was doing or what characterization he was aiming at from reading and learning these isolated pieces of dialogue.

For your second audition, it is a good idea to come dressed more or less for the part. If the character is conservative—a serious-minded young teacher or secretary—don't come in frills and ruffles or a miniskirt up to your thighs. Wear the most sensible shoes you have, plain stockings, and make sure your hair is neatly arranged.

Of course if you are reading for a part in a costume play no one expects you to have a Victorian outfit, but it is a good idea to comb your hair in a way to give you a period look. Usually you will have been given just overnight to study the script, but this is ample time, especially if you have had someone cue you as you will be cued in your audition.

I have heard some brilliant readings given in auditions. In the old days of radio plays, it was extraordinary how well young people read even at the first audition because they were trained to sight-read for the microphone. Oddly enough, though, most of them never improved beyond audition level: they gave shallow, off-the-top-of-the-head performances and were unable to round out the characterization.

Like most directors and producers with long experience in the theatre, I have developed almost a sixth sense about talent. I know almost at once—sometimes after the first few words, and often before the words are spoken—whether or not an actor will ever measure up to the necessary performance.

I never need to audition an established performer to make sure he is right for a new role, but since I am not always able to convince the author or composer or musical director or the others connected with one of my productions, I go through the audition routine for them. I am always very pleased, of course, when my selection turns out to be right. Some stars refuse to audition for a role and are insulted that they were asked to. They feel their work is well known and that a producer should know whether they fit a specific role.

You may be called back several times and asked to read with other members of the cast. The final audition is apt to be on a stage, and that will be easier for you because most of your judges will be out in the darkened auditorium. Besides, by this time the director of the play will have started working with you, not only in order to help you toward a proper performance but to discover how you react to his direction. Do exactly as he directs, without question.

If after all this you are not engaged, do not despair. Your time and efforts have not been wasted. The director will remember you and you will have gained considerable experience.

Rehearsal

On the other hand, if you do get the part, be happy but not complacent. Even after you have signed your contract and have gone into actual rehearsal, there are still five days in which you can be replaced.

It is very important that you memorize your lines as quickly as possible. The director really cannot begin to tell much about your ultimate characterization and performance if you must keep your head buried in the script.

If you are a college graduate and accustomed to cramming for examinations, you should be able to have the script out of your hand within two or three days. It is a good idea to exer-

cise your memory every day by learning a poem or a Shakespeare soliloquy. Most young people have no difficulty with
their lines. Their trouble comes more from inability to create
and hold on to a characterization.

Joining Equity

One of the most important things your first job does for you,
whether you keep it or not, is to give you the opportunity of
becoming a member of Actors' Equity. Over and over I have
heard the cry, "I can't get a part unless I belong to Equity,
and I can't belong to Equity unless I have a part. What do I
do?"

Obviously 15,000 members of Equity got into the union by
some means. In order to get an application to join, you must
have an Equity contract from a producer. Though producers
often will say that they will see only Equity people, this is
just their way of limiting the auditions; they often see non-
Equity talent, with the understanding that, if you get the role,
you will become a member.

As soon as you get your contract, you go to the office of
Equity at 165 West 46th Street. The Information Center will
direct you to Membership for your application.

There is a general misunderstanding that one can become
a member of Equity by being an apprentice in a summer stock
company. This is only true after you have served a first year
of apprenticeship. In that first year, you can play an unlimited
number of roles as a nonmember. In your second season you
can play three roles without membership, but if you are fortunate enough to be given a fourth role, you will not only be
allowed to become a member of Equity, you will have to
join.

Equity designed these rules so that the summer stock management couldn't use your talent indefinitely without putting

you under Equity contract and paying you an equitable wage.

The fee for joining Equity is two hundred dollars. This is a lot of money to pay all at once, but occasionally the producer will pay it for you and deduct it gradually from your salary. Since the Actors' Equity minimum in summer stock (based on the lowest potential gross per week) is $90.00, even during rehearsals, you won't receive less than that, no matter how small the role you are to play, so a deduction of fifteen or twenty dollars a week will not be a hardship for you. Minimum based on the highest potential gross in summer stock is $120 per week. (Broadway minimum is $145 plus cost-of-living increase; road minimum is $195 plus cost-of-living increase. This is for both dramatic and musical performers.)

Advantages of Equity

Aside from the protection it offers, Equity acts as a sort of club. When you go there, you meet other theatrical personalities, even stars; it is an excellent place to make contacts. It actually should be the first place you stop off each day before making the rounds, since Equity lists all the casting needs for all shows produced on Broadway.

Seven days prior to notifying agents of the characters needed for casting a production, the producer must notify Equity and send a breakdown and description of the characters. These lists are posted on the Equity bulletin board, together with the time and place auditions are being held.

There is an exception. When the producer must have certain stars or when the playwright has written the play with certain stars in mind, such stars may be hired before the Equity call, but this information must be on the list when it is sent to Equity in order to cover understudies.

The director often tells the actors he already has in mind to attend the general Equity call; although they are the ones who get the parts, the other actors who try out are not wasting their time: if they make an impression on the director, he will remember them for another production—or try them in a different part in the same play.

In the case of a musical, there are Equity calls for "male singers," "male dancers," "female singers," and "female dancers," and again no casting in these categories may be done until these calls have been attended to.

Formerly Blacks, Orientals, and actors from other ethnic groups came to Equity calls only when the cast list specifically required them, but as there is less and less discrimination in the theatre (there never has been any at City Center), more talent is coming to the auditions from these groups.

There are "open calls" (open to nonmembers of Equity) for off-Broadway and off-off-Broadway productions, but there are no such open calls for Broadway productions.

The Equity Library Theatre

The Equity Library Theatre has been in existence for over twenty-three years. It is nonprofit, sponsored by and receiving some financial aid from Actors' Equity, but most of the budget comes from "'patrons of the arts" and fund-raising activities.

The Equity Library Theatre presents ten major productions a year as well as a production for children, at the Master Theatre, 103rd Street and Riverside Drive, averaging one play every five weeks from October to May. Each has a different director, cast, and crew.

The range of plays is from musicals to dramas to comedies: the Rodgers and Hart musical hits of the 20s; *The Visit*, Friedrich Dürrenmatt's drama; Ibsen's *An Enemy of the People*; *He Who Gets Slapped* by Leonid Andreyev; Susan Slade's *Ready When You Are, C.B.*

It provides a professional showcase for actors, giving young performers the opportunity to display their talents. It has produced over 470 plays, showcased over 9,000 artists, and played to over half a million people. It is guided by such artists as

Ralph Bellamy, Maurice Evans, Lloyd Nolan, Cornelia Otis •
Skinner, Sam Jaffe, and it has been a steppingstone for such
artists as Jason Robards, Jr., Tony Randall, Kim Stanley, Eli
Wallach and Anne Jackson, to mention but a few.

Rita Gam became a member of Equity through her first
performance at City Center in José Ferrer's dynamic production of the Kapek play *The World We Live In* (or *The Insect
Comedy,* as we called it), in which Joe cast her as a butterfly
because of her beauty, and because it was not a speaking
part.

One day when she was making the rounds, she walked into
the Equity office and was immediately cast in their production of the restoration play, *A New Way to Pay Old Debts.*
After that Equity called her again to play the nurse in their
The Hasty Heart. It was then that she decided to study seriously and enrolled in Harold Clurman's dramatic class, which
led to starring roles in television and films.

The Equity Library Theatre is unique and the best outlet
for producing professional plays as showcase productions; they
play to invited theatrical VIPs who are in a position to hire
talent.

5. Education for the Theatre

Today there is no excuse to arrive in New York totally unprepared for a career in the theatre, whether it be for acting, directing, stage designing, or whatever you have in mind, because theatre arts and crafts are being taught in hundreds of universities and even in many high schools.

Some of the courses are inadequate and some of the teachers have had no contact with the professional theatre, but still taking a course in drama will teach you many of the fundamentals: how to study a play and analyze the characters; how to memorize a role quickly; how to fit words to action; how to project your voice without shouting; and, most important of all, how to work with others intent on a career in the theatre—academic or professional—without self-consciousness. Even poor basic training is better than none and the earlier you start, the younger you will be when you feel ready.

That feeling of being prepared is all-important because it gives you confidence, and confidence in yourself, in your ability and what you have to offer to the world is an enormous asset. To reach that point of confidence, you must have a trained and disciplined mind, body, and voice.

The more education you have, the better your mind will be. As I have said, it is not difficult for young people to memorize lines, but I have found that college graduates with some experience in stage work are much quicker and more accurate in assimilating character and inner meaning when given a part to read "cold" than are those without college training.

The study in depth of English, speech, psychology, history, philosophy, and music is all grist to your mill. If your school or university doesn't have a separate drama department, it is almost certain to include the study and analysis of plays in some of its English courses.

In researching this field, I have discovered that there are over one thousand universities and colleges giving dramatic courses, so if you have always had a bent for theatre work, there seems little excuse for your not attending one of them, and I have included a list of many of them in the back of this book.

Yale, New Haven, Connecticut; Carnegie Institute of Technology, Pittsburgh, Pennsylvania; Northwestern University, Chicago, Illinois; Baylor University, Waco, Texas; University of California, Berkeley and Los Angeles; Stanford University, Palo Alto, California; University of Hawaii, Honolulu; University of Michigan, Ann Arbor; University of Minnesota, Minneapolis; University of Dallas, Texas; Trinity University, San Antonio, Texas (linked with Dallas); University of Washington, Seattle; New York University, New York City, are outstanding among these, and many of their graduates have become highly honored professionals.

In attending university drama classes, you make valuable contacts for your future career. Professionals in all theatre fields are invited to visit these drama departments to share their knowledge and experience by way of lectures and demonstrations and sometimes to participate as actors or directors.

Often the school dean becomes a good friend of these professionals, and when you graduate and go to New York he can give you a letter to one of them.

University Theatre

"It is no longer any disgrace to have studied theatre at a university," says Professor Wilson Lehr, Director of Theatre at Brooklyn College. "Really, it is only within the last ten years that this has become apparent. When I was graduated from Yale with a Master of Fine Arts, I never mentioned it when I tried to get a job. Not that I was ashamed of it, but in those days, few actors or directors had studied at a school of fine arts which had a theatre program and while a university degree was not exactly a handicap, it certainly was no asset in breaking into the theatre."

University theatres operate in three ways, depending upon the people who are in charge.

Types of University Theatre

1. The conventional university theatre uses undergraduates, graduate students, and even faculty to put on a season of plays —perhaps four or five—and relies exclusively on talent available on the campus. It replaces the old-fashioned dramatic club presentations which were "coached"—never directed—by someone in the English department, and the extracurricular play, sometimes called the Varsity Show, usually put on by the senior class and coached by a theatre-minded faculty member or student. Fumbling and amateurish though these productions were, some real talent came out of them. Rodgers and Hart started working together with a Columbia University Varsity Show, and many other important people in the theatre (Joshua Logan, José Ferrer among them) came out of college shows. But they were what they were called—amateur theatre.

The university theatre today is no longer an extracurricular affair. It is a professional course of study, and a major subject leading to a degree. The theatre building is usually a modern workshop, beautifully designed and equipped and heavily subsidized. The productions are attended not only by the university body and faculty but by the community. In fact, most university theatres with subscription series draw heavily from the public. Some of them have "invitational series" for which they bring in a professional company, such as Judith

Anderson in a special production of *Medea,* as a community project. The students are not involved in these plays at all.

2. A university will frequently invite a star or a well-known director to head a campus company for a semester. Stars and directors of the highest magnitude enjoy working with students in an academic atmosphere for a short period of time. The students receive excellent training under this arrangement, and the star and/or director benefits by the prestige of having been invited to do this work.

3. The big thing at the moment is the university theatre with a resident company; that is, one or two professional directors with a minimum technical staff and a small company of Equity members move onto a campus, live there, and, under the auspices of the university, present a season of plays in which the students participate.

Advantages of University Theatre

It is a great advantage for students who are studying theatre to be working with professional craftsmen. This merger of the professional theatre and the university is an ideal one but, like all marriages, even perfect ones, it has drawbacks. One of the biggest is that the professional group may take over the production and leave the students on the sidelines, using them for small and unimportant parts, if at all.

Even so, the director usually feels that the contact the student has with the professional is more valuable than the part he plays or the technical work he performs.

Donald Madden is an excellent example of the university-trained actor. While he was a student at City College, New York, he appeared in about every play given, and there was no job too small for him to perform. He wanted above all else to be an actor—to be in the theatre.

When he finished college, he took no further acting courses or training. He made the Broadway rounds, got into community theatre (where he received no salary), and went anywhere that he had a chance to act. Then he had two years in the Army where he managed the G.I. Theatre.

His Army service finished, he returned to making the rounds, his interest in theatre stronger than ever. He saw every play in which there was a part he thought he might be able to do. He appeared in university theatre plays without pay and was given roles in Sartre and Shakespeare. During the summer he worked in summer stock for room and board.

His Broadway break came when he became the understudy to Kenneth Haigh who played Jimmy in *Look Back in Anger.* It was an all-British company, but Donald worked on the accent and no one ever guessed that he was born on Amsterdam Avenue in New York City.

When Kenneth Haigh left the play, Donald stepped into the part. He has been kept busy in a number of plays since then, but he says he will not accept a role he feels is not right for him, preferring to wait even though it may mean hard financial times for a while.

Since his major role in Peter Shaffer's play *Black Comedy* on Broadway, he is on his way to become a big star. Donald was hailed by the critics for his versatility in this production. In the curtain raiser, *White Lies,* he was a Cockney tough. In *Black Comedy,* he played a London swell of dubious gender and he was hilariously funny. He played both parts to perfection.

Acting Classes

There are many excellent drama classes you can attend in New York in which you will meet not only newcomers like yourself but veterans, even stars. All too often the wait between engagements is a long one even for well-established actors, and they keep themselves sharp by attending classes.

Stars and unknowns work happily together in these groups and workshops. You needn't be backward about speaking to established players and telling them about yourself, your aspirations, and your special talents. If the impression you make is a strong one, and they notice that your work is outstanding, they might recommend you to a director or producer friend of theirs.

Uta Hagen, Sanford Meisner, Robert Lewis, Gene Frankel among others have important classes.

The American Academy

The American Academy of Dramatic Arts, 120 Madison Avenue, New York 10016; Phone: MU 6–1944, offers a two-year course, and on request will send their catalogue, describing the curriculum. To join the Academy, a personal interview is required, as well as two letters of reference—character and financial. You must be a high school graduate and send a transcript of your record. You also need a doctor's certificate filled out on a form provided by the Academy.

After you have filled out the application forms, you will be given an audition by the director of admissions plus one or two other members of the administration or faculty. They will ask you to do two scenes, both monologues, one comic and one dramatic. They have a booklet of scenes to show you what they are looking for.

You are not required to have previous experience; they will accept anyone with the proper qualifications and talent. The first year, consisting of twenty-eight weeks, starts in October and classes are scheduled four hours a day, Monday through Friday, either mornings or afternoons.

The second year is almost exclusively dedicated to the rehearsal and production of full-length plays presented with scenery, lights, costumes, and make-up before a professional audience. Rehearsals are regularly scheduled in the second year, four hours a day, Monday through Friday, between 2:00 P.M. and 6:00 P.M. All other training activities average a minimum of five hours per week.

American Academy of Dramatic Arts production of *David and Lisa*, featuring John S. Youngs and Katherine Irving. *(Lee Owens)*

For students who work during the day, night classes meet twice a week from 6:30 to 9:30 P.M. and the course consists of six terms of approximately three months each.

There are also two summer sessions, one consisting of three-day-a-week classes and the other of five-day-a-week classes.

A number of scholarships are available and the income from several funds affords partial assistance to outstanding students with financial need.

Only about one-third of the class is invited to continue in the second year. The work is more intensive; actual plays are prepared for the Academy's showcases.

Agents, directors, producers, talent directors for films and casting directors for television, sponsors of the Academy and others are invited to these showcases and several times recently participants have been engaged immediately.

Cleavon Little was one of these. He went directly into *MacBird*, off Broadway, then into *Scuba Duba* and Joseph Papp's *Hamlet*. He was also engaged for two films, *What's So Bad About Feeling Good?* and *The Detective*.

Another graduate, Kathy Burns, received the Clarence Derwent award for her outstanding work in *The Prime of Miss Jean Brodie*. Both of these young artists are "types" or "characters" but both have enormous natural ability and the proper training to express it.

More than a score of American Academy alumni from recent classes are working not just in New York but all over the country —on tour, in resident companies and in "packages." The list of American Academy stars is like a *Who's Who* in the American theatre: Charlton Heston and Ossie Davis, 1948; Kim Stanley, 1949; Rod Steiger and Martin Balsam, 1950; Jason Robards, Jr., 1955; Marlon Brando, Paul Newman, Shelley Winters, Geraldine Page, Dustin Hoffman and many, many others.

Actors' session of Actors' Studio. Lee Strasberg
(second from left) is part of the audience for Shelley Winters
(third from right). *(Syeus Mottel)*

The Actors' Studio

To get into the Actors' Studio, 432 West 44th Street, New York 10036; Phone: Plaza 7-0870, you must already be a professional player, and you must apply in person. All they ask is your name, address, and phone number. You are not questioned about your experience, and you are scheduled for one of the preliminary auditions which are held every two weeks.

You are required to do a five-minute scene with another person of your choice. (The scene must not be from Shakespeare.) The three judges for these auditions are chosen by Mr. Lee Strasberg, the Studio's founder and artistic director, from the directors, playwrights, or actors who are members of the Studio.

If you do not pass the first audition but still show some talent, you may be asked to do a second audition. You will be given an idea of the kind of scene you should do—what would show off your particular talent best. When you come back for the second audition, the Studio will try to have at least one or two of the same judges who heard you the first time.

Final auditions are held twice a year. At that time you are judged by the directors of the Studio and by all those who were judges at the preliminary auditions. If you pass the final audition, you are eligible to join a class.

Over a thousand auditions are held each year, and from these not more than five or six actors are accepted as new members. Membership is for life, completely free. The Studio is supported by donations, many of which come from members who have become great stars—including Anne Bancroft, Marlon Brando, Sandy Dennis, Julie Harris, Anne Jackson, Paul Newman, Sidney Poitier, Rod Steiger, Eli Wallach, Shelley Winters, and Joanne Woodward.

There are about 370 members of whom about 100 are usually active at the Studio. Because of the abundance of talent brought together, the climate is very stimulating and creative.

Regular classes are held twice a week under the direction of Lee Strasberg, the man solely responsible for the Studio's artistic management since 1949.

Both Mr. Strasberg and the Studio have reputations that border on legend, and both have been centers of controversy since the beginning. The famous "Method" is Mr. Strasberg's personal approach to the ideas of Stanislavski on acting and directing, and the Studio is a way of life for many theatre people. While many young actors swear by "The Method," there are many others, especially among the older and established stars, who swear at it.

During the sessions, new members are presented, and their work is criticized by their fellow actors. They learn to use their initiative and to organize experimental projects. The Actors' Studio also offers a speech teacher and classes in fencing and body work.

6. Broadway

Even when you are hired, it may be some time before you are called for the first day of rehearsal if casting is still going on, but don't worry. The call will come either by telephone from the stage manager, or by mail or telegram, and you will be told where to report and when.

The first day of rehearsal is an exciting one. It probably will start at 10:00 A.M. Don't be late! A representative from Actors' Equity will be there to make sure that all the players, stage managers and the director are paid-up members and have signed contracts. He will take care of the cards covering all the deductions, fringe benefits, etc., and make sure the actors elect an Equity deputy for the run of the show. The members may vote for a deputy, but usually the Equity representative suggests one of the older members of the cast who has acted in this capacity before.

The deputy acts as liaison between management and equity. Any complaint an actor has against management is given to the deputy, rather than direct to Equity; similarly, any complaint management has against an actor is given first to the deputy.

When all of these details are out of the way, the director will call everyone together for what I consider one of the most interesting and thrilling moments in the production of a play —the first reading. It may be the first time you have a complete script in your hands and the first time, too, you will hear the complete play.

You will be grouped in a semicircle, facing the director, the playwright, stage managers, and probably the producer. Read well; do your very best. Many actors have been replaced from this first reading and their "runners-up" taken instead. This first reading is the orchestration of the play. The voices, the thoughts behind the playwright's words, must blend, must build to the proper points, must find the humor or pathos of the lines, must bring the playwright's intention into focus.

Several times I have been at a first reading which I felt was the best performance the play ever received. This was certainly true when I produced Chekhov's *The Cherry Orchard*, starring Helen Hayes, for television. If only that first reading could have been the final taped performance, it would have been in my opinion the greatest Chekhov ever presented. Alas, in breaking it up into bits and pieces for the camera, the flow, intensity, and sheer delight were lost. This also can happen in the theatre where scenes are individually rehearsed, piece by piece, and never somehow fitted back into the original pattern.

The Rehearsal "Pattern"

Some directors spend the entire first week on reading and discussion of the play: the playwright's intentions, the characters and their development, the underlying motives and ultimate resolution. This approach usually appeals to the younger members of the cast and those with an academic approach to theatre, but makes the older, experienced actors very nervous.

Fredric March said to me once, "The last time I rehearsed for a play, we didn't rehearse; we just sat there talking until I finally said to the director, 'Hey, this is all very interesting but I'd like to know where I am going to be on the stage when I'm thinking all these deep thoughts as I try to remember my lines!' "

Other directors, usually the older ones, put the company on

its feet after the first reading and start blocking the action—telling the actors where to go and what to do—immediately.

If you disagree with your director's system, don't let him know it, especially by taking a bored or indifferent attitude. No matter how small your role is, don't start knitting or doing crossword puzzles—although it is important always to have a pencil and paper handy for noting changes and corrections in the script—until you have learned not only your own lines, but the complete scenes in which you are to appear.

Unless the play, the company, and the director are so exciting that they hold the attention at all times, rehearsals can become rather boring for the actors with bit parts. A good director will, therefore, call only the performers he wishes to work with on certain days and give the others the opportunity for costume fittings, photographs, hair styling, or just time off.

But try to be present at all rehearsals even if the director says it isn't necessary, because this is better than going to classes. Watching a good director work is a valuable course in theatre.

It is very unprofessional as well as impolite to get into a discussion with another actor when you are out of a scene but in the same hall or room. Even whispers are very distracting to the director and the other actors who are trying to concentrate. Also it is not a good idea to discuss your characterization or conception of the role with another actor. If you have any problems, take them up with the director. He will be only too happy to help you. Do not be timid about asking the director questions about lines, even about words which are not quite clear to you in the early days of rehearsal. However, if you have a major point of characterization to discuss with him, wait until the general rehearsal is finished so that you can take it up in private.

Don't be self-conscious during rehearsals. No one is judging you or expecting a miracle at that stage. You are working with your peers. No outsiders are allowed at rehearsals.

Years ago when I was doing publicity for Rachel Crothers' play *When Ladies Meet,* which was rehearsing on the stage of the John Golden Theatre where I had my office, I crept silently into a seat in the last row of the theatre to watch Miss Crothers at work. I sat there in the dark, fascinated, without stirring or making a sound, yet suddenly she whirled around and said, "Someone is watching us. Who's out there?"

Miss Crothers was a good friend of mine, and I had done the press for several other plays of hers so I had no compunction in calling out my name.

"Get out!" she roared. "You should know better! A rehearsal is as private as taking a bath."

Not all directors are as sensitive as Rachel Crothers was, but rehearsals all are very private affairs.

"Personality problems" is a phrase I often hear actors use, and it is a fact that now and then violent dislikes among the cast crop up during rehearsals and can be disastrous to the project. They are to be avoided like the proverbial plague but, if that is impossible, then it is up to the producer and the director to try to keep some semblance of peace. And it is best for the actors not involved to keep as aloof as possible.

Once the run-throughs of the play start, everyone in the cast must be present just as for an actual performance. It is a good idea to dress attractively and appear at your best at this time for you never know when the press agent for the show will turn up with a photographer to make rehearsal photos. Only the stars will have advance warning. But if you catch the photographer's eye, you may get your picture taken, too!

Tryouts and Previews

A straight play usually has four weeks of rehearsal before opening out of town for several weeks. It is during tryouts of a new play that much of the grueling work of rewriting starts;

Susan Sullivan, Pamela Payton-Wright, Charles Siebert, and Dustin Hoffman during a pause in rehearsals for *Jimmy Shine*. *(Friedman-Abeles)*

not only lines are changed but often whole scenes, even whole acts. This is all terribly disconcerting to inexperienced actors. Scenes they have carefully worked over for weeks are peremptorily dumped, and whole new scenes, with just enough of the old lines retained to make the scenes doubly confusing, are put in to be played at once with virtually no rehearsal. I have heard actors say, "We never play the same scene twice out of town or at the previews," but incredible as it appears, it seems to work, for many great successes have developed in just this tortuous way.

Even if the play turns out to be a smash hit, and runs on and on, you will not be free of rehearsals; they are frequently called for the sake of the understudies and cast replacements. Then, too, many producers and directors insist upon periodic run-throughs in order to keep the play up to the sharply defined performance of the opening night, for actors often start "reaching for laughs" (exaggerating their readings or gestures) or actually changing the lines either through faulty memory or because they think that they can improve on the author's work.

Out-of-town tryouts are very expensive and so the custom of giving two or three weeks of preview performances in New York, at the theatre in which the play is to open, has become more and more popular.

These long periods of previews are possible today because the New York critics will review the performance which the producer designates as the official opening night, but not too many years ago the critics insisted on covering as an opening any first performance for which the public bought tickets.

Opening Night

Even after you go through all the necessary preliminaries of training, striving, auditioning, and finally getting a part, and then through all the tedium, long hours, frightful hard work and nerve-racking changes in the role, you may find yourself in a state of emotional despair only an hour or so after what might really have seemed to you a triumphant first-night. For opening night audiences can be very deceiving. The investors' friends and the relatives of the cast will be out front making a valiant effort to whoop it up—laughing and applauding at any possible opportunity in the hope of influencing the critics. These demonstrations, I believe, may sharpen what might have been so-so reviews into scathing ones.

The opening night party has become a tradition. The cast, the investors, stars from other current productions, celebrities in general, and newspaper columnists are invited if it is to be a big blowout such as Alexander Cohen often gives in the Rainbow Room, sixty-four stories above Manhattan in Radio City. There is usually an orchestra for dancing and several bottles of champagne are in ice buckets at every table.

The Sardi Club on the second floor of that famous theatrical restaurant on 44th Street is taken over for the more conservative parties. In the case of a City Center production party, this is strictly "Dutch treat" since we are a nonprofit organization and cannot spend our donors' money on fripperies. But in general the opening night party is usually included in the production cost and paid for by the management of the play.

It is at this party that the first critical reviews are heard from the television critics who, in one or two minutes, can help make a hit or ring the death knell. At Sardi's, several copies of *The New York Times* are brought in as soon as the edition with the review comes off the press. (*The Times* has a back door almost next door to Sardi's on 44th Street.)

In the case of parties taking place in the Rainbow Room, the Plaza, the St. Regis Roof and other favorite spots, it is the press agent who brings in the paper. Sometimes even before the review is printed, he has called the city desk and had the review read to him.

If you are at the party and do not see or hear the review itself, you will know at once whether the review is good or bad by the immediate reaction of jubilation or stunned silence.

For me there is no more heartbreaking moment in the theatre than when a happy group of players and backers who are sure they have a hit cease to celebrate.

Several times recently, preview performances have been sold out to enthusiastic audiences. Yet the day after an official opening and poor notices by the critics, there have been cases when not one ticket was sold, and the company has found itself playing to just a handful of disgruntled theatregoers who bought their tickets in advance.

In such a case, it is a kindness on the part of the producer to close the play at once, not only to save himself and his investors considerable money, but to spare the sensibilities of his actors.

If you are fortunate enough to become associated with a repertory company in New York—the APA-Phoenix or the Lincoln Center Repertory Theatre—bad reviews will not be catastrophic, because these companies operate on subscription systems. The Lincoln Center company has been pounced upon, mauled and kicked about three times out of five, but despite the critics it still flourishes with an extraordinary attendance record.

City Center Productions

Since we choose only masterpieces of the American repertoire for our musicals at City Center and have been able to recruit superlative performers, we have been kindly treated by the theatre critics. We find, however, that "kind" reviews are not enough and only outright raves—"Run, do not walk"—"If you miss it, you're a masochist"—"Far better than the original and that was perfect"—cause a real flurry at the box office.

But whether the reviews are kind or raves, we must run our

Pierre Olaf and Victoria Mallory rehearse for City Center's Christmas, 1968, production of *Carnival*. *(Friedman-Abeles)*

allotted scheduled time—usually three weeks. Sometimes we lose as much as $35,000 or $40,000 a week when the public doesn't respond, but unlike a Broadway production, we cannot close. On the other hand, we have the help of the five thousand Friends of City Center, who each subscribe from $15 to $1,500 a year.

If the production is a real smash, we cannot extend our engagement because another company is already in rehearsal for the next show which must open on the specified date. If the final production of our spring season of musicals is a hit, however, it can be extended. We did this with two shows, *Carousel* and *Pal Joey*.

We maintain a very rough schedule for our revivals, especially for the elaborate musicals. Only two rehearsal weeks are allotted for musicals and plays, and so everyone must work at top speed and concentration.

The incumbent attraction closes on a Sunday night, as our week starts on Tuesday (no "perfs" Monday, as the theatre ads put it). This means that our stagehands sometimes work all Sunday night taking out the sets and properties of the previous production and bringing in the new ones. They set them up Monday and have them ready for a technical rehearsal at seven o'clock that night.

These Monday nights are usually headache time for all concerned. It is the first time the actors will be in costume, makeup, and working with the scenery and properties, and the first time the stage crew will be making the set changes. Also the lighting director will be out front doing his work—giving the light cues to backstage electricians and to the spotlight men who are stationed way up at the back of the second balcony. He will have a headset and be talking into the mouthpiece, but if it is that unique lighting genius, Abe Feder, his stentorian voice will reverberate through the empty auditorium and often burst forth like a sudden clap of thunder.

The actors will pay not the slightest mind to this or to the usual backstage racket of falling scenery, dropped props, and accompanying expletives.

Out of all this chaos comes enough of a performance for the director to make certain changes in the positions of the cast. Even though the cast has followed a floor plan in the rehearsal halls, working with the actual scenery points up problems. Hoopskirts must be made to negotiate narrow doorways, groupings can look crowded or unattractive; often whole scenes must be moved closer to the footlights to accommodate the acoustics of the 3,000 seat house.

This is the first chance, too, that we out front have to see the actors in make-up and costume—full costume if we are lucky! Since we have new costumes for each production, sometimes all of them are not finished in time for Monday night. If I hadn't had twenty years' experience with this situation, I might panic, but after all this time, I know the costumes will be ready for the actual dress rehearsal Tuesday afternoon because our costume designers, wonderfully gifted and completely reliable men, assure me of this and I trust them. I have to—the play must open Tuesday night!

7. Away from Broadway

If your first role is in summer or winter stock, and the play you are engaged for is a revival of a past success, rehearsal time is very brief. You start playing for an audience more often than not in one week or less, and no time is lost by the director.

After a quick first reading, he immediately starts blocking the action and before the end of the second day, you are on your feet and have a pretty good idea of where to go. By the fifth day, run-throughs start and you are expected to be letter-perfect, for on the sixth day there probably will be a dress rehearsal before an invited audience. On the seventh day you open!

Fortunately for young actors and actresses, there is enormous activity in the summer theatres which now number well above a hundred. Many of these theatres have resident companies and a great majority of them take on apprentices for the season, sometimes paying them a small salary, or sometimes charging them for the opportunity.

Either way, it is a rewarding experience, for apprentices are given the opportunity of doing just about everything: helping to paint and build the scenery, scouring the neighborhood for the loan of furniture and props, selling tickets in the box office, and ushering. And of course now and then they even get to act—but not often.

If you are hired as an actor, however, you will get to act

all right; you will rehearse one play all day and play a different one that night. However, you probably will not be called upon to play a young person in one play and an octogenarian in another, for typecasting has become the rule. Your make-up may change, but it must be almost imperceptible.

Make-Up

The art of applying make-up used to be a very important one for actors, but very little make-up is used in the theatre today. With so much emphasis on typecasting, a heavy street make-up is about all the women use, and most men use none at all or just a bit of foundation to make them look healthy or pale as the role requires. False eyelashes have done away with the use of cosmetique—the waxy mascara which used to be heated and applied with a little stick to "bead" the lashes.

Repertory companies must depend on make-up to some extent because with only a certain number of actors in the company, typecasting is not always possible and the actors must "age" themselves or change their type in order to fill the roles.

These make-up changes if not done very skilfully are distracting to today's audience, used to television and motion pictures in which make-up is never apparent. TV and the films have developed highly skilled make-up artists, and when really necessary they are pressed into service by theatre companies.

Probably the most exciting job of make-up in recent years was done by the company of *The Persecution and Assassination of Jean-Paul Marat as Performed by the Inmates of the Asylum of Charenton Under the Direction of the Marquis de Sade*. Each inmate of the asylum was an outstanding and unusual example of the mentally disturbed. Virtually everyone wore a wig in a state of great disarray. Some of the faces were distorted; warts and odd-shaped noses were everywhere.

Samuel Liff of the David Merrick office tells me that a special make-up man traveled with the company, carrying with him a small kiln in which he baked, with some sort of plastic material, the various protuberances which had to be made new for each performance. But this kind of make-up is a rarity.

Near Broadway

There are three important legitimate theatres within less than an hour's drive from Broadway which function all year round and while they usually play packages or take an entire show after it has closed on Broadway, they sometimes produce their own plays or musicals.

The Playhouse-on-the-Mall in Paramus, New Jersey, run by Robert Ludlam and situated in the midst of a huge shopping center, is one of them. The theatre is completely modern with very fine backstage facilities including excellent dressing rooms. It has a loyal and enthusiastic audience and is highly successful.

The Mineola Playhouse in Mineola, Long Island, has had its ups and downs but at present is embarked on its most ambitious project: the Plumstead Theatre Players, organized by Martha Scott. Martha, who was the original Emily in Thornton Wilder's *Our Town,* selected that play as their first offering and put together an extraordinary company for it: Henry Fonda, Robert Ryan, Estelle Parsons, and Jo Van Fleet, just to name a few.

The Paper Mill Playhouse in Millburn, New Jersey, was founded by the late Antoinette Scudder and Frank Carrington in 1934. It was opened to the public in 1938, after the old mill had been converted into a modern theatre. It was established to prove that a live theatre can be successful in an average American community if it presents good plays.

The Paper Mill Playhouse has had no subsidies or gifts beyond the money raised initially for the buildings and presents Broadway successes as well as original productions of its own.

The first reading of *Our Town* by the
Plumstead Theatre Players, Mineola, Long Island.
Left to right: Henry Fonda, John McGiver, Estelle Parsons,
Jo Van Fleet, Robert Ryan, Karan Kay. *Back to camera:*
Director Edward Hastings, from the
American Conservatory Theatre. *(Friedman-Abeles)*

During the early years of its existence, Miss Scudder under-wrote some of the more costly productions. An average of fifteen to twenty productions a year, one third of which are musicals, are presented.

Mr. Frank Carrington, the founder-director says, "We get our actors from all the usual sources in New York, but we take anyone who has professional standards and talent." Mr. Carrington holds auditions in New York at the Showcase Studios, 950 Eighth Avenue, and he also has an office at 330 West 45th Street, New York 10036; Phone 265-3995.

Summer Theatre

There is a booklet published in the early spring called *Summer Theatre* which you can buy at any of the newsstands in the theatre district, or you can get it by mail by writing *Show Business*, 136 West 44th Street, New York 10036. This lists just about every summer theatre in the country and gives details such as whether or not the theatre books in "packages," plays semipackages, has a resident company with a guest star policy, or depends upon its resident company completely.

The Package Deal

A package is actually a complete company which travels from theatre to theatre doing the same play and touring with everything except, in most casts, its scenery which is constructed and painted in each theatre. In a semipackage, designed for a play with a large cast, only four or five of the featured players travel together; local players fill in the other roles, or actors from New York are "jobbed in" to round out the cast.

A rather delicate operation is called for with the semipackage. An advance director-stage manager keeps one week ahead of the booking, rehearsing the resident actors or jobbers-in in their roles; when the featured players arrive, he puts the two parts together, hopefully with happy results.

It may not seem possible, but usually the results are good even with only one or two run-throughs of the play. There have been times, though, when the featured players were forced to arrive late and to go on with no rehearsal at all. This is pretty nerve-racking to everyone concerned, including, in my opinion, the audience.

The visiting star system works quite well, as the star usually allows a full week to rehearse with the entire company. But if the star is playing a part he has been doing on and off all summer with various companies, he may arrive only in time for the dress rehearsal, thereby creating a situation similar to that of the semipackage plan.

In all of these various forms of summer theatre, each theatre has a separate contract with the actors, pays their salaries and also their traveling expenses. Usually the theatre has permanent arrangements for dwelling places for the visiting companies, and the advance man and/or local manager tells the arriving actors of these places to live.

Being in a package show is a delightful way to spend a summer, since most theatres are located in pleasant resorts. You usually have only one weekly rehearsal, often the opening day, in order to acquaint yourself with the new set of scenery, and there is plenty of time for swimming, tennis, golf, and other summer enjoyment.

Winter Stock

Winter stock, as it is now called, is mainly in the South, and it is not "stock" at all as virtually every play has an entirely different cast, often rehearsed in New York. The productions are given at the Coconut Grove Theatre in Miami, the Parker Theatre in Fort Lauderdale, or the Royal Poinciana Theatre in Palm Beach, often as a tryout for their worth as a Broadway attraction.

These Florida theatres lure some very important stars for some pretty terrible new plays, but since the theatres have virtually sold-out subscription seasons, it doesn't seem to make much difference. The audiences see the stars they enjoy, and the producers save themselves a mint because the operators of the theatres pay most of the cost of the production and all of the salaries. If the theatre owners like the play being tried out—and they usually do or they wouldn't book it in—they often insist upon being a co-producer should the play turn out to be a hit and go to Broadway.

Resident Company

The resident company works together as a unit for ten or more weeks in the same theatre. It is grueling work, for you are rehearsing one production while playing another, and you have virtually no time off, but the results are often superior theatre. There are many resident companies with no "names," which play to packed houses because of the excellence of their offerings. It is with a resident company that you get your finest experience. It takes a disciplined mind indeed to absorb *Death of a Salesman* in the afternoon's rehearsal and play to the laughter of *You Can't Take It With You* that night.

8. Repertory Theatre

If you have the good fortune to be engaged as a member of a repertory company, and you have the talent for it, you are on the way to becoming a real protean actor. There is, however, very little true repertory in the United States because the cost of mounting a different play every night—like the cost of opera and ballet repertory where different works are given each night—is incredibly high.

Some American repertory companies—very few—manage to do two or three different plays in a week but the majority of these companies, such as the one at Lincoln Center, New York, produce one play and run it for several weeks before changing to another play; they try to present their most successful one at the tail end, hopefully for a run.

Years ago when Gilbert Miller brought Laurence Olivier and Vivien Leigh to Broadway to do *Antony and Cleopatra* one night and *Caesar and Cleopatra* the next, he found the cost so backbreaking, even with sold-out business, that he was forced to change the schedule to four consecutive performances for each play each week.

Even the Old Vic, which was a true repertory company in London, was forced to adopt the American pattern of a one- or two-week run for each play. Of course this is also easier on the actors, as it is mentally and physically exhausting to play an entirely different role every twenty-four hours, especially without a prompter.

The prompter's box is a familiar sight in most of the European repertory theatres, but it is not used here. When the Moscow Art players were at City Center in New York, they were appalled at the lack of this—to them—all-important piece of stage equipment and insisted that one be hastily constructed. It was discovered that there was no way to cut a hole in the "apron" where they wanted the box to be put because of the steel beams under the stage at that point, but some sort of arrangement was finally concocted rising out of the orchestra pit.

The Metropolitan Opera House has the only prompter's box I have seen in New York. In fact, they use two prompters there—one to remind the singers of the words and music and the other to indicate the action or stage direction. It seems incredible to theatre people but opera singers—even stars—sometimes give a performance without ever having rehearsed with the company.

The Case for Repertory

It is really too bad that true repertory is virtually impossible in the United States, because for young actors the difficult work gives the kind of finish and technique which is never learned in drama school or acquired by repeating the same part in a long-run play. There is the lure of a whole season's work, and of financial security of a sort (although repertory companies pay notoriously low salaries), but the main thing is the opportunity for playing many and varied roles.

As a matter of fact, the plea for repertory in this country doesn't come from the theatre-going public, but from the actors themselves: they instigate and lead all the campaigns we have from time to time.

Eva LeGallienne always believed in the repertory system and headed the famous Civic Repertory Company on 14th Street. She was praised steadily by the critics, but steadily lost money until she was forced to close many years ago. Miss LeGallienne also headed another company, The National Repertory Theatre Company, which spent much of its time touring the country and was seen in New York for several short seasons, but it too could not weather the financial storms and was disbanded after an expensive season at the beautifully restored Ford's Theatre in Washington.

Repertory theatre is bound to be a losing proposition. All of the great companies of the world—The Comèdie Française, the Old Vic, the Royal Shakespeare, the Piccolo Teatro di Milano, the Moscow Art Players, the Brecht Company in East Berlin have been, and always will be, heavily subsidized by their governments.

For the first time in the history of this country, there is a general move toward subsidy from our government through the National Council of the Performing Arts of which Roger L. Stevens is the Chairman. Although millions have been appropriated for distribution, this country is so vast and performing arts groups are so numerous—there are one thousand symphony orchestras alone, besides ballet companies, opera companies, resident grass-roots theatres, all desperately short of cash—that probably there never will be enough to satisfy all needs. However what money has been available has been wisely spent, especially in certain emergencies such as when the American Ballet Theatre Company received $250,000 which enabled it to survive.

What is known in show business as the critics' pet repertory company—The Association of Producing Artists, now the APA-Phoenix Theatre—was founded in Bermuda in 1960 by its president and artistic director, Ellis Rabb. In 1962, the company gave its first New York season at the off-Broadway playhouse, the Folksbiene, with a repertory of three plays, *The Tavern, The School for Scandal,* and *The Seagull,* all directed by Mr. Rabb and all highly successful.

The Phoenix Theatre Company, headed by T. Edward Ham-

bleton and founded by him in 1953 jointly with Norris Hough-
ton, had held out at the large Phoenix Theatre on Second Avenue and 12th Street for eight years, had made many friends,
and had produced some resounding hits such as *Once Upon a
Mattress* and *The Golden Apple,* but had lost over a million
dollars. In 1964, Phoenix presented APA at the off-Broadway
East 74th Street Theatre. The merged company became an
immediate success with excellent productions of *Right You
Are, The Tavern, Scapin, The Lower Depths, War and Peace,
Judith,* and *Man and Superman.*

The combined APA-Phoenix took over the Lyceum Theatre
"on Broadway" and had the good fortune to start right out
with a smash hit—Kaufman and Hart's *You Can't Take It
With You.* At this writing they are in the midst of their fifth
season at their large and comfortable new home, doing excellent business, still gathering critical acclaim—and losing money!

However, during their 1966–67 successful season at the
Lyceum, the Ford Foundation gave them a three-year grant of
$900,000 on condition that it be matched by $450,000 of other
contributions each year. The National Council on the Arts
granted them $250,000 of this amount for two years.

The APA-Phoenix moves out to Ann Arbor in the fall where
they do a season in combination with the Professional Theatre
Program of the University of Michigan, headed by Robert C.
Schnitzer.

The third and well-entrenched group is the Lincoln Center
Repertory Company now at the Vivian Beaumont Theatre.
This company has had so much publicity—most of it adverse—
ever since its inception in 1963 that it needs little mention
here. The company started off with two remarkably gifted
directors at its head—Robert Whitehead and Elia Kazan. With
the Vivian Beaumont Theatre way behind its completion
schedule, and an excellent company already formed, the Anta
Theatre in Greenwich Village was hastily constructed through
the good offices of Robert Dowling and New York University.

Taken in retrospect, their first season was brilliant. It opened with two new productions by eminent American playwrights—Arthur Miller's *After the Fall* and S. N. Behrman's *But for Whom Charlie*—and a very beautifully costumed revival of O'Neill's *Marco Millions.*

After the Fall was controversial (should Arthur Miller have disclosed so much of his own life, especially in relation to his second wife, Marilyn Monroe?) and received mixed notices. Nevertheless it was a success. The Behrman play was criticized for the casting of several parts—the same actors who had been praised for their performances in *After the Fall.*

This is the danger of repertory with a small company. All of us, including critics, have become used to typecasting, and unless the company goes outside its ranks it will find itself forced into the old stock-company pattern of putting a white wig on a young actor or expecting a dramatic leading lady to carry off a sophisticated comedy role.

Marco Millions is a beautiful play but too long, too overwritten for today—and Mrs. O'Neill allowed no cuts.

Mr. Whitehead and Mr. Kazan started their second season with an experiment, a seventeenth-century Jacobean melodrama, *The Changeling,* by Thomas Middleton and William Rowley, which was a critical and financial disaster, and led to the replacement of these two gifted directors. The season ended with an extraordinarily fine production of *Tartuffe,* directed by William Ball.

The Vivian Beaumont Theatre finally completed, two young men who had been running the critically acclaimed but deficit-ridden Actors' Workshop in San Francisco—Jules Irving and Herbert Blau—were brought to New York with virtually all of their semi-amateur company to replace the brilliant and sadly maligned Mr. Whitehead and Mr. Kazan and their young but too small (too small because of economics) company of gifted and established players.

The results, as expected by the pros but not by the public

which bought up 39,000 subscriptions, were far less successful artistically than the Whitehead-Kazan seasons.

Mr. Blau has since resigned and Mr. Irving has been driven to desperate measures to rescue his company. He has invited in "guest stars" and even gone so far as to add outside and definitely Broadway commercial productions—Lillian Hellman's *The Little Foxes,* directed by Mike Nichols, and Brian Friel's *Lovers* starring Art Carney.

The engagement of Margaret Leighton to play the South Carolinian, Regina, in *The Little Foxes* in the 1967–1968 season, and the casting of Anthony Quayle as guest star in *Galileo* that same season, caused a furore among the American players; pickets at Lincoln Center protested the engagement of these two English stars by what had originally been hailed as an all-American repertory company. The new Equity contract reached after the two days' actors' strike of 1968 includes stricter controls on casting of aliens.

William Ball, after his tremendous success with *Tartuffe,* went on to form his own repertory group, The American Conservatory Theatre, and found a home for it in Pittsburgh where he achieved a fine artistic success—praise from the press and the intelligentsia—but incurred the usual large deficit and was soon dispossessed. After considerable wandering and gigantic fund-raising efforts by Mr. Ball to keep his company intact, he eventually found two homes: one in San Francisco for twenty-two weeks and the other in Chicago for twenty weeks.

The first of the successful United States repertory companies was in Minneapolis at the specially built Tyrone Guthrie Theatre, opened in 1963. Sir Tyrone Guthrie had made his international reputation as administrator-director of the Old Vic in London and as the first director of the Shakespeare Festival at Stratford, Ontario, Canada. His debut in the theatre was as an actor with a repertory company.

As long as his repertory group included major stars such as Hume Cronyn and Jessica Tandy, business was excellent, but little by little deficits increased and the company had to be rescued by a Ford Foundation grant.

Regional Opportunities for Newcomers

With the rise of the numerous and excellent regional theatres, many of which have adopted the more currently favored title of repertory theatre, you may find that your opportunity for a professional career lies close at hand.

If you are fortunate enough to be offered work in one of these organizations near your home, accept it at once, no matter how unimportant the post may seem to you. The first step, the breaking-in, the joining with the professional theatre is the most difficult. Even if you are to be a lowly gopher (go-for coffee, go-for props, go-for costumes), it is a start, and that's what you need.

It doesn't matter much whether your ultimate aim is to act or stage-manage or direct or produce; any connection at all with the professional theatre should be welcomed. You can always learn, and the more you absorb about all phases of show business, the better equipped you will be to deal with your own part of it and the more at home you will feel.

Theatre Communications Group

So closely connected in fact are these regional theatres to Broadway, that a special organization called Theatre Communications Group, 20 West 43rd Street, New York, nonprofit-making and supported by a Ford Foundation grant, acts as a liaison, particularly from the casting point of view, between them and the New York acting pool.

There is no membership fee for actors. You register with the Group, and you stop in regularly to see what is available. The directors of the regional theatres call on the Group when they need actors. If a special type is requested, the Group consults its files, picks out someone they feel fits the requirements, sends out a call and arranges for the actor to meet the director.

If actors are hired locally by a regional theatre, they apply for Equity membership by mail as soon as the contracts are signed. There are regional actors, members in good standing of Equity, who haven't been in New York for years; they go from one regional theatre to another while waiting for the call to Broadway.

These regional theatres have replaced the stock companies which used to flourish throughout the country and which gave opportunities to many talented local performers.

There is a great difference, however, between the old-time stock companies which depended upon popular Broadway successes, especially melodramas and comedies, and the modern regional theatres. The latter concentrate on classical drama and avant-garde plays from all over the world, and turn to an occasional Broadway success only as a change of pace for players and public. Most of the regional theatres are set up as nonprofitmaking organizations and are supported by local contributions (tax deductible), generous grants from the foundations, and, recently, government subsidies.

All of them require a dedicated director—one like Margo Jones, who before her tragic death was director of the theatre in Dallas that now bears her name, or Zelda Fichandler of the Arena Stage in Washington, D.C., or Nina Vance of the Alley Theatre in Houston.

9. Television and Radio

Television

Hollywood used to claim that "stars are not born; they are made" through publicity campaigns. Motion picture stars still profit from these gigantic exploitation projects, but in television, the public makes the star, sometimes overnight.

The sudden flash of a new talent on home screens brings an immediate reaction and a demand for further appearances. This, of course, is the exception, not the rule. However, stars— at least drawing cards—are being made every day in "prime time" at night on popular series or on the special guest programs such as "The Tonight Show," "The Merv Griffin Show," "The Joey Bishop Show," and the vaudeville shows such as "The Ed Sullivan Show," "Hollywood Palace," "The Las Vegas Show," etc.

Then, too, there are the daytime soap operas, although the favorite heroes and heroines of these never seem to become really big stars.

Originally New York was a fertile television field for talent, but currently production here has dwindled and there are about a hundred times more programs being produced on the West Coast. In New York, the reliance is still on tape; in a very few instances, the programs are "live."

In the wonderful days of the Columbia Broadcasting System's "Studio One," "The DuPont Show of the Month," "The

Lux Video Theater," "Playhouse 90" and "The U.S. Steel Hour," programs were televised "live." I can't think of a more difficult or nerve-racking experience for the actors—to say nothing of the producers, authors, and directors—or a more exhilarating experience for the viewer. Cameras and actors strove for perfection and often achieved it.

The so-called "live on tape" programs (I never understood this term but have been told it means "without cuts or retakes") lack the urgency and excitement and occasional booboos of those great old days.

Soap operas, however, are still done live and offer magnificent experience for young players. The necessity of memorizing a half-hour show every day gives the player a knack which rarely deserts him.

But the underplaying necessary for television work is sometimes hard to overcome when the stage calls. Stage work is larger than life; television work on that small home screen must, of necessity, be smaller. However, a really talented actor automatically adjusts to either need.

While, as I said, television producing is done mostly in California today, there are still many opportunities in New York. The most lucrative work is in commercials.

A glance at the pages of *Show Business* or at Jerry Leichter's *Ross Reports*, published by Television Index, 150 Fifth Avenue, New York, N.Y. 10011, will give you an idea of how many advertising agencies have their own casting directors. It is a good idea to send a photo and résumé to every one of them.

When the listing doesn't particularly specify "photos and résumés only," you can take a chance and make a personal call.

If you get as far as an audition, always remember that you are on the "smaller" stage. Do not overact or overproject your voice. Be as natural and charming as possible, and above all, use very little make-up. Simple clothes and hairdos, and a fresh, scrubbed, well-pressed look are best.

Television Production

There are several important producing organizations, but their status changes from month to month. The only way to keep informed of their activities is by subscribing to the Bible of television information, the aforementioned *Ross Reports*, which is published monthly and lists the New York advertising agencies, producers of commercials, active "package shows" using live talent and film, television talent agents, literary agents handling TV scripts, network and local station producers, addresses and personnel managers of network offices and studios.

It is just as difficult to get that first job in television as in the theatre. Sending in a résumé and photo is important. Some conscientious producers do file them after examining them, and frequently if you have an arresting face—not just a pretty or handsome face—you will get a call, because they are always on the lookout for interesting new types.

That Elusive "First" Job

Personal contact in television is important, and if you can get in to see the producer or director you can sell yourself much more effectively. Here the young actor must use the same ingenuity and perseverance he would use to get into the theatre: make the rounds, try to meet TV people at cocktail parties and places where TV people congregate.

William Fowler, playing the juvenile lead in my summer touring company of *What Did We Do Wrong?*, started as an actor by doing television commercials. His interest in the theatre began when he was a little boy in Winnetka, Illinois. Having three gifted sisters, all painters, Bill said he had to do something of an artistic nature to get attention in his family and he began to play-act everything he did. Then, too, his father, an advertising executive, had done some acting and so further stimulated Bill's interest in the theatre.

He was fortunate in attending a high school in Winnetka that had a very good dramatic department and a roster of distinguished stars who had studied there: Ralph Bellamy, Charlton Heston, Rock Hudson, Hugh O'Brian, and lovely Ann-Margret with whom Bill appeared in a school play.

After graduating Bill attended the University of Chicago and studied speech and speed reading, and from there he went on a round-the-world voyage of the University of the Seven Seas for a semester, during which he had the opportunity of studying the folk music of the twenty-two countries the floating university visited.

When he returned, he entered the American Academy of Dramatic Arts in New York and was graduated from the two-year course. During that time his family paid his board and tuition, and until he began earning money, he lived at the Madison Square Hotel at 26th Street and Madison Avenue. It was inexpensive ($80.00 a month) but he shared the bathroom with nine other roomers.

Someone at the Academy told him about an opportunity to audition for a commercial for a new Howard Johnson product. Bill was given the part and although the product didn't "take," Bill did. He continued work in a number of commercials by studying the lists of the agencies in *Ross Reports*, and then making the rounds and meeting the agents.

Another book which gave Bill names and addresses of television opportunities is *The Madison Avenue Handbook*, published by the Peter Glenn Publishing Co., 145 East 53rd Street, New York, 10022, and available by mail and at most major bookstores.

A friend of Bill's father who was with the J. Walter Thompson Advertising Agency opened other doors, and Bill met Edward Robbins of the William Morris Agency who cast him in his first summer stock job in *The Impossible Years* and in a "package" the following summer. Bill then spent three years with the Summerset Players in Winnetka, playing in *Come Blow Your Horn, The Matchmakers, The Pajama Game, I Remember Mama,* and others, and so Bill was well launched on his theatrical career.

Television Agents

In New York you can get a part without an agent; in Hollywood it is impossible. Hollywood still operates on the Screen Actors Guild dictum that no one without an agent will be seen. So if you go to Hollywood and want to be in television, your first task is to find an agent to handle you.

You can ask several agents to represent you simultaneously. They then split any commissions. Commissions are set by law and are based strictly on 10 percent of the AFTRA (American Federation of Television and Radio Artists) scale. All agents in New York and California are franchised and work under the same laws as employment agencies.

Agents are supposed to guide you, and many of them do, but some cannot (unless you are a star) because they don't have time. This has led some actors to take on personal managers. But some of these managers work outside of the law and take as much commission as they can get—sometimes as high as 40 percent if their client becomes a star—and since they usually demand a seven-year contract, a personal manager can end up as a real liability for an up-and-coming actor.

It is just as difficult to get a good agent to handle you in New York as it is to get a television job there, but the usual procedure in New York is for the agent to seek you out; the more promise you show, the better agent you are likely to attract.

Opportunities

There are no hard and fast rules on how to break into television. Every success story is different and the difference between success and failure can be accidental. Some make it, some don't. Even if you have talent, success—particularly in television—depends on many unknown factors: being in the right place at the right time; being photogenic; being the kind of personality that stands out; being the particular type a producer happens to be looking for; and being just plain lucky. And contacts are of course important. Television is full of cliques and it is a good idea to be part of one.

Radio

The opportunities in radio are far less. There are virtually no chances for real "acting." Disc jockeys, now called "air personalities," are usually engineers. If you consult the "help wanted" columns in *Broadcasting Magazine,* you will see that most such jobs call for engineers; in fact, the F.C.C. demands this if they are one-man operations: putting on the records, manning the microphone, and working alone with only relief help.

The best place to start in radio is in a small town, although the wages are notoriously low. You work for peanuts, but you do get experience that way. If you have an outstanding speaking voice and have put in an apprenticeship as a one-man or one-woman radio personality in a small town, you still must pass a speaking test to do the same kind of work in New York. The test is given by all the broadcasting companies to determine whether you have any speech difficulties and how your personality comes through.

Radio commercials offer about the only acting possibilities. Here, of course, your voice is more important than how you look or how good an actor you are.

Just about every station has an interview program which offers other openings. In New York City there are a number of them, like Arlene Francis and her "Luncheon at Sardi's," which has been on the air for years and years. Martha Dean,

Jack O'Brien, Joe Franklin, Sandy Lesberg, Mary Healy and Peter Lind Hayes, Barry Farber, and others have interview programs. They all need people to line up their guests, for instance. Some have a staff furnished by the station; others personally engage assistants.

While having a program of your own may be a remote possibility, being connected with one in any capacity is interesting work and a source of countless contacts, which, as I keep insisting, are the most important things to have in all branches of show business.

Radio today can't actually be considered part of your career in the theatre though television definitely is. While the technique *is* different, the requirements of appearance, experience, and diligence are the same but your very own personality—even your own character—will be the final deciding factor in either field and magnified as it is by that candid camera-eye, it is even more vital to you in television.

Joining the Union

As in the theatre you must join a union. For television and radio, the union is the American Federation of Television and Radio Artists. You can be engaged for a first job without being a member and then join up as soon as you sign a contract; as in Equity, you can pay your membership dues in installments. The initiation fee is based on income and all fees are clearly defined in the AFTRA Code of Fair Practice booklet. The office in New York is located at 724 Fifth Avenue, New York 10019. AFTRA minimum salaries are standardized for every type of performance, with strict rules governing rehearsal time, minimum calls, etc.

If you work in both theatre and television or radio simultaneously, there is a reduction in your initiation fee. If you are a member of Equity, you pay half of the Equity initiation fee of $200—$100—to join AFTRA. Yearly dues can be sus-

pended if you do not perform in television or radio for a specified length of time, if certain conditions are met. All conditions and rules are for the benefit of the performer, and all
questions will be fully answered by the AFTRA office.

Part Two: Musical Theatre

10. Today's Song and Dance

From *The Black Crook,* 1867, to *Promises, Promises,* 1968, the musical has been the glamour girl of American show business —and always the most expensive to produce. It is also considered the biggest risk. The musical through the years has paid the largest return, however, and along with jazz has become known as one of the only indigenous American art forms.

While a straight play begins and very nearly ends with the playwright, the musical is a true collaborative effort of many talents. It is dependent to a great extent upon the basic theme or book, but it is also needful of memorable music, fine lyrics, original choreography, beautiful and appropriate costumes, novel and/or exciting settings, and a firm overall directorial hand to provide a strong and united whole.

Then there's the casting, which is as important to success as it is in a straight play. The cast for a musical calls for specially gifted and highly trained performers, not only for the principal roles but also for the ensembles. Unbalanced casting can have disastrous results. If the leading players have been selected for their names rather than for their abilities, and an actor in a minor role stops the show with a brilliant dance or an exceptionally well-delivered song, it is usually more harmful than helpful to the overall effect of the musical. Sometimes when this happens during the out-of-town tryout, the star or stars demand the removal of the performer who is, in their words, stealing the show, and then they attempt to perform the hit dance routine or audience-pleasing song themselves. Sometimes this heartbreaking rearrangement works out for the overall good of the show, but not often.

An Equity casting call for a straight play at City Center often brings us several hundred applicants for the few roles that are open. But when we have an Equity audition for our musical productions, for which we need twenty singers and twenty dancers for the chorus alone, we are fortunate to have eighty to a hundred applicants in all, and there are always many more girls than boys. The reason for this is pretty clear; there are many many more Equity members who can "just act" than there are those with the special training and discipline which singers and dancers must have for the sort of ensemble work we have come to expect in modern musicals.

Each season the standard of training and skill for performers in musicals seems to rise. We have been fortunate lately in being able to find twenty exceptionally fine dancers in a single audition. In the final choice, height and appearance play their part; dancers are chosen because they are a certain type while others, equally skilled, lose out because of an inch or two one way or the other.

Fine voices are harder to come by for us because at City Center we have always been more particular about our singing ensembles than is the average Broadway producer, and our choral directors are much more demanding. Only highly trained voices are used.

I put all this emphasis on ensemble work because undoubtedly that is the way you will start if your aim is to work in musicals. And wonderful work it is, too—hard, grueling, demanding—but in the end exhilarating and rewarding. To be even a tiny cog in the intricate machinery of a successful Broadway musical is to have—as some young players tell me— a taste of paradise.

Voice Training

If you have an especially good voice, it will take you far, but only if it is properly trained and used. There have been a few great "natural singers," of whom Ethel Merman is an outstanding example, but most of the other men and women who have reached the top and stayed there through decades—Mary Martin and John Raitt, for example—have trained their voices to achieve that priceless effect of freshness, naturalness, and apparent lack of effort so pleasing to listeners.

Listeners, whether they realize it or not, participate in a singer's efforts, and if the singer strains, the listener strains, too, and is made uncomfortable. When Joan Sutherland hits a high E flat with the greatest of ease, her listeners break into applause and cheers because they, too, have miraculously hit that incredible note! I actually have had a slightly sore throat after listening to a singer with a poorly trained voice struggle through a song recital.

If you have a pleasant voice, your family has probably seen to it that you have been given some instruction, but you should continue with your lessons, no matter what the sacrifice. They are vital.

But singing lessons alone are really not enough if you are going to make a career in the musical theatre. The trend today is to use singers who can dance and dancers who can sing, and so body training is highly important and acting classes are, too. As I said in the beginning, musicals call for highly trained and highly skilled performers. The day of the beautiful but dumb chorine has long since passed.

The old-time sugar-daddy backer of a musical who used to insist upon a producer putting his current ladylove in a leading part is no more—unless the lady in question happens to be a highly qualified performer.

I had such an experience. One of my backers in a Broadway show suggested a young lady for a certain part. We were both pretty surprised when I said, "She's the one I already cast in that part!" I had known nothing of their intimate relationship.

Dancing Lessons

If you are interested in being a dancer, you probably had ballet lessons as a child; if so, I hope you have continued them as ballet is the perfect base on which to build. A beautifully trained body can easily adapt itself to the various schools of dancing: those of Agnes de Mille, Jerome Robbins, Michael Kidd, Peter Gennaro, Gower Champion or, of course, Balanchine.

The quality of ensemble dancing in musicals has steadily improved since 1943 when Agnes de Mille first startled Broadway with a full-length ballet in *Oklahoma!* danced mostly by members of her own company.

Jerome Robbins' dances in *West Side Story* were another milestone. Gower Champion has been a bright innovator and so have Bob Fosse, Michael Kidd, and Oona White.

But there are times when a return to the past rather than an innovation is in order as in *Walking Happy*, which had a British background. Choreographer Danny Daniels brought back old-fashioned time steps and clog dancing, executed with astonishing skill and precision.

"I sent out a call for dancers who had a tap-dancing background or who had studied tap-dancing in their early years," Mr. Daniels explained. "It wasn't easy to find them because tap-dancing is a relic of the past. [Before de Mille!] All the boys I selected had formerly studied tap. One of them, Al Lanti, had taught tap steps in England where they are still popular.

"It was because they knew tap that they could execute the steps that comprised the clog dance. Clog dancing and tap-dancing are very akin to one another. I used the old-time clog dance as a basis and theatricalized it."

Pierre Olaf *(sixth from left)* and dancers of City Center's
Carnival rehearse Mr. Olaf's famous number, "Cirque de Paris."
(Friedman-Abeles)

If you were inventing a young dancing star for a story, you couldn't dream up a more perfect girl than Sandy Duncan, who, at this writing, is twenty years old.

"When I was six," Sandy told me, "I went with my mother to a dance rehearsal in Tyler, Texas, my hometown. During the performance, I was so excited, I ran down the aisle and tried to get on the stage to join in the dancing. My mother retrieved me, of course, but when we got home, she said that if I wanted to dance that much, maybe she ought to send me to dancing school.

"She did and I adored it. When I was twelve, my dancing teacher brought me to the Dallas Summer Theatre to audition for a role in *The King and I.* I was given the part of one of the children, but I danced in the adult ballet, 'The Small House of Uncle Thomas.' Then, while I was in high school, I worked in the Dallas theatre every summer. It became almost like home to me."

One summer the director brought Sandy to New York with him so that she could audition for plays while he looked for talent for his summer theatre. Gus Schirmer, who remembered seeing her in Dallas, put her in *The Music Man* at the City Center.

Sandy's dancing teacher had originally come from New York and, before Sandy left home, her teacher arranged for her to live at the Rehearsal Club where Sandy stayed until she married recently.

While still playing in *The Music Man,* Sandy rehearsed with a touring company and when *The Music Man* finished its City Center run, Sandy went on tour playing in *Bye Bye Birdie, Gypsy,* and *Brigadoon* in St. Louis, Kansas City, Pittsburgh, Chicago and smaller cities.

An agent from the William Morris office signed Sandy the first week she was back in New York, and he enrolled her for dramatic lessons in Wynn Handman's acting school. He also sent her to Sue Seton, a voice teacher. Sally continued dancing on her own. Each summer she went back to summer stock.

Sandy has appeared with distinction in *Life With Father* and was outstanding in *Finian's Rainbow* and *The Sound of Music,* all at City Center. She played in the off-Broadway hit, *Your Own Thing.* Before that and because she felt the experience would be valuable, she went on a U.S.O. tour of Vietnam in my production of *Guys and Dolls* with Hugh O'Brian who played the role of Sky Masterson at City Center.

TV commercials and industrial shows pay Sandy well enough for her to continue studying, perfecting her skills, and preparing for the big break that will make her a star. When it comes, she'll be ready for it.

(She was ready for it, and has just opened in a big, Broadway musical, *Canterbury Tales,* in the leading ingenue role. Her reviews are excellent.)

All-Around Training

Though there have been excellent schools of acting for many years, until recently there was no school devoted to the training of performers for the musical theatre.

When Philip Burton, the foster father of Richard Burton, arrived in this country from England in 1962, he almost immediately saw a need for this training. With financial support from a group of dedicated theatre lovers, Mr. Burton created the American Musical and Dramatic Academy (AMDA) located at 245 East 23rd Street, New York 10010. Among its patrons are Richard Burton and Elizabeth Taylor, of course, and Marge and Gower Champion, Carol Channing, Dina Merrill, Sammy Davis, and several wealthy "lay people" associated with some aspect of theatre, mostly as backers.

The two-year training program starts in September and is divided into four semesters each lasting sixteen weeks. The Academy also has part-time courses and evening courses. In the full-time course approximately thirty hours of instruction are given each week in acting, speech, rhetoric and verse-speaking, dramatic literature, individual voice instruction, sight-singing, musical theatre styles, eurhythmics, dance (modern, jazz, and period), fencing and make-up. Individual singing lessons are a particular feature of Mr. Burton's Academy. Two private lessons a week are given to every student.

All applications are by interview. Mr. Burton has no auditions, for he considers them misleading. Those too far away for a personal interview can apply by mail, but everyone must have the recommendation of someone Mr. Burton respects.

"I give all singers an ear test," Mr. Burton says, "to make certain they aren't tone-deaf." They don't call it that any more, by the way. The singer now claims he has a "pitch problem." Mr. Burton says he can tell immediately in an interview if the applicant has such a problem, in which event he is ineligible.

The American Academy

The American Academy of Dramatic Arts, 120 Madison Avenue, New York 10016, does not have a course specifically listed as Musical Comedy, but among the fundamentals taught at the Academy, dancing, singing, and mime are stressed. According to Miss Frances Fuller, Director of the Academy, the basic principles of acting are the same in both dramatic and musical theatre. The performers who demonstrate ability in Shakespeare generally have an equal aptitude in musical theatre—provided, of course, they can sing and dance. While the students learn acting, those who have good voices or dancing ability and can afford special instructions are encouraged to study singing or dancing privately.

For the past thirteen years the Academy has been putting on full musical productions as part of its regular schedule. These productions are given with costumes, lights, and sets, in theatres and before audiences. All have top directors and professional choreographers and musical coaches. Milton Greene has coached the singers for the last five or six years and accompanies them. A good three-piece orchestra can do wonders.

Constance Towers, Florence Henderson, Louise Troy, Eileen Brennan, David Hartman, and Jim Luisi are only a few of the many Academy alumni who have won recognition in musical theatre.

The Manhattan School of Music

The Manhattan School of Music is planning an extensive training course for the musical theatre, but cannot inaugurate it because of lack of space until the Juilliard School of Music moves to its new quarters in Lincoln Center, so that the Manhattan School can take over the old but roomy building at 120 Claremont Avenue. At this writing, the faculty for the new course is being assembled and the various programs outlined.

The Manhattan School of Music is one of the finest musical institutions in the country. Its training course for light opera and musicals will undoubtedly rank very high.

Auditioning

If like Sandy Duncan, you have started dancing and/or singing lessons at an early age, and there is a summer tent or musical theatre in your hometown or conveniently nearby, it is a good idea to attend any of the theatre's calls which are open to nonmembers of Equity. But when you go to such an open call, be aware that you may not be given a chance to audition. The first "screening" is for the selection of the proper types, and there is no point in the director's wasting your time and his own if he is looking for dark Latin types and you are a tow-headed, fair-skinned appleblossom of a girl or boy.

Also, don't take it personally or feel you haven't had a proper opportunity if you are permitted to sing only a few bars—in fact, haven't really been given a chance to get going. The musical director knows exactly the kind of voice he is listening for, and again it is a waste of time to have you continue if he knows your voice doesn't fit the requirements.

Unless you are extraordinarily fortunate, you will be rejected many times, and so it is a good idea to develop a philosophy (or a thick skin) about rejection at an early age. Always remember *all* auditions are completely objective from the director's point of view. He is thinking only of the overall success of his show. Even the smallest mistake in casting can destroy the perfection he must look for.

If, however, you are asked to return, do so in an assured, businesslike way. If you are a dancer, a leotard is the best uniform. Be sure you have the proper shoes: ballet slippers are best for most of the dances choreographed for Broadway today. If you are a girl with long hair, wind it up and tie it securely, unless the role expressly calls for it loose. (Very seldom.) A mass of hair—even beautiful hair—flying about is distracting.

Listen carefully to the dance director's instructions and watch carefully when he illustrates the steps you are being asked to execute. He will probably want basic technical patterns. Depending upon the type of show it is, the patterns may be from ballet, tap, or modern. Sometimes a show uses a combination of these and so the more dance training in all these fields you have, the better for you. Tap, as I have said, is rarely used these days—more's the pity.

The longer you have to wait, and the more dancers you can watch audition, the better off you will be when your turn comes. If you can find a spot, it is even a good idea to practice along with the music. Don't be embarrassed about this. No one will object and the dance director will be grateful if you prove adept.

When your turn comes, do your best with confidence and a smile. Have a happy expression. A grim look of determination is not very attractive. Remember that though now your only audience is the dance director, in the final analysis your goal is to please an audience.

If you are auditioning as a singer, make sure you are simply dressed and that your hair is neatly arranged away from your face. If you have bangs, please, please avoid the present tendency of allowing them to tangle with your eyelashes.

If you are auditioning for an original musical, you may be called upon to sight-read a brand-new song, and so although you will have the help of an accompanist, it will be to your advantage if you have been trained to sight-read. It is, however, not absolutely essential if you have a beautiful voice, well placed and produced, because most music directors rehearse songs by rote. As long as you don't have a tin ear or, as Philip Burton puts it, "a pitch problem," you can do very well.

More usually you will be asked to sing music with which you are familiar, and a copy of which you are to bring with you. Pick something simple to show the quality and range of your voice. Do not act out the song or make unnecessary gestures. It is not your acting that is being tested right now, but your ability to do the sort of singing necessary for the show. Do not pick Gershwin's "Summertime," an excellent song for showing off a lyric soprano, if what is needed is a "belting" or chest voice. You probably will be told the type of song required, but if not, make sure you find out.

Don't worry too much about your first audition. You will learn fast and act like an old pro after two or three attempts, whether or not you are accepted.

Rehearsing for Musicals

If you are selected, and are called for rehearsal, the routine will be more or less the same whether it is for a new Broadway show or an out-of-town revival. Everything I have said about rehearsals for a legitimate play applies to the musical theatre also, but the schedule is quite different.

Dancers, singers, and principals rehearse as separate groups, in different rooms, each group with a piano and pianist. In the case of a new show, the singers and dancers may have no idea what the story line is or how their numbers will fit in until the first run-through. In the case of a revival of a well-known musical, it is taken for granted that you are familiar with it. But you can always ask the overall stage manager or his assistant for a script. He will be happy to know you are interested. Personally, I always insist that everyone know what is being done and why.

You will rehearse seven out of eight and a half hours each day except for the final week before the opening when Equity permits a workday of ten out of twelve hours.

If you are a dancer, come to rehearsal in ample time to allow for putting on your work clothes and taking a warm-up period. (If you are a singer, warm up at home!)

The choreographer will begin by demonstrating the steps to a series of counts—one, two, three *and* one, two, three *and* bend, etc.—sometimes to music but very often without. It is by endless repetition of these patterns that the dances eventually evolve. After the steps have been learned, absolute precision in their execution is the requisite.

Don't try to show the dance director what a high kicker you are if a shoulder-high kick is all he calls for. There can no longer be any show-offs in the ensemble.

It certainly was quite different years ago. I remember particularly going to see the *Greenwich Village Follies* when I was co-producing and directing vaudeville skits. My partner, Dan Jarrett, and I had been looking for a young actor who could dance, but we had had no success. Then that night we spied a red-haired adorable lad who was knocking himself out in the chorus line. We immediately went backstage and hired him. That started quite a career for Jimmy Cagney.

Gypsies

"Gypsies" is an affectionate nickname for the members of the ensemble. There is an amusing tradition among them that

Rehearsal of a scene from *Zorba'*, the Broadway musical starring Herschel Bernardi and Maria Karnilova. *(Friedman-Abeles)*

Dance rehearsal of the Broadway musical, *Promises, Promises*.
The musical numbers were staged by Michael Bennett.
(Friedman-Abeles)

apparently started back in 1950 when an ensemble dancer in *Gentlemen Prefer Blondes* presented a satin dressing gown to a "gypsy" friend in *Call Me Madam* on her opening night. The "gypsy" who received it gave it to another friend in the ensemble of *Guys and Dolls* on *its* opening night, and since then the now famous "gypsy robe" has been handed on from one musical to another.

If you become a gypsy, you will enjoy yourself if you are gregarious, easygoing, and happy. You will be in close contact with a greater variety of personalities than you ever dreamed existed. Generally the entire female ensemble has one large dressing room lined with mirrors and make-up shelves; if you are lucky, you will have about two feet of a shelf to call your own. Firm friendships can come from these close quarters, but not if you are fussy, touchy, and unhappy without privacy.

If you need privacy, you won't get far as a gypsy in or out of the theatre. For the close quarters continue even when the performance ends for the night. On tour with a musical it is usual for two, three, or even four people to share one large room. And in New York an apartment is frequently shared as protection against that catastrophic moment when your show abruptly closes—perhaps after the opening night. Your roommates then can help carry you until you find another part or another source of income.

Remember, then, that desire to be in the theatre, even extensive training for it, is not enough to guarantee success or happiness in it. Your background, personality, ego, and temperament are important elements in your destiny.

How They Got Started

The question that is asked most frequently of stars and other successful personalities in the theatre is "How did you get started and how did it happen?" Two friends of mine have been good enough to tell their stories.

Angela Lansbury, who electrified Broadway as a musical comedy star with her brilliant performance as Mame in the smash hit, said there is no substitute for dramatic training for the aspiring actor or actress. This is true whether for a straight play or a musical comedy today. Good characterization is almost more important than singing and dancing ability for the leading roles in *My Fair Lady, The King and I, Carousel,* and almost all of the "classics" including *Mame.*

"Although I was exposed to theatre all my life," Miss Lansbury said, "since my mother was an actress, I nevertheless went to dramatic school in England when I was a child and when I came to New York, I continued my training at the Feagin School of Dramatic Art.

"While I was there, I was coached by a young man who thought I'd be good in night clubs. In 1942 he put together an act for me which was a special arrangement of a song which Beatrice Lillie did years before called 'I Went to a Marvelous Party.' I'm not sure who wrote it; Noel Coward possibly.

"In the adaptation that my friend Arthur Bourbon concocted, I gave a variety of musical impressions of people with different accents. Arthur hired a rehearsal hall for two dollars an hour and rehearsed me in my act until he felt I was ready. He then asked an agent friend of his to handle me. This man called me up and asked how I would like to do an audition at Roseland; he had a client coming down from Montreal who owned a night club there and who was looking for talent. He thought I, being English, might appeal to Canadians.

"Well, I had the audition and I got the job. It paid sixty dollars a week and my fare to Montreal and back. I had to lie about my age; I said I was nineteen. Actually I was barely sixteen, but I needed the money badly. My mother and twin brothers and I were evacuees from England and money was scarce.

"I was very green and terrified, but I did the act and enjoyed the experience. It was really my first professional job in show business. The engagement was for three weeks, but it was extended for two weeks beyond that, and it was really quite successful.

"Right after that I went out to California to look for a job in motion pictures. It was quite different in those days. All the studios had starlets who were terribly pretty—beauty contest winners, orange queens, rose bowl queens—and most of them had very little dramatic training. The studios used to provide coaches to teach them how to act.

"I was a *rara avis*. I was young, healthy—though beauty was not my forte—and I *could* act. Nevertheless I couldn't get by the doormen at the gates of the studios. What finally happened was that a friend of mine was being considered for the role of Dorian Gray and he mentioned to the director that he knew a young English girl who was a good actress and who happened to be in California, but couldn't get inside a studio.

"My friend arranged for me to see Albert Lewin, the director, and he was very kind indeed, but he didn't give me a part in his picture right away. But, the casting director took me to see George Cukor who was doing *Gaslight* and I made a test for the role of Nancy, the maid.

"It was a successful test except that the powers-that-be decided I was too young for the role; but since I showed promise as an actress, they signed me to a contract. Within a week they changed their minds again, and I got the role of Nancy in *Gaslight*, and subsequently I got the part of Sybil Vane in *Dorian Gray*."

When musical comedy stars were being considered for *Mame*, and it was realized by the authors that the part called for a strong acting performance, the authors' agent remembered Miss Lansbury's ability as a night club performer, and so, rather to the surprise of Broadway, it was she who was given this superstar-making role, probably the "fattest" part since Mary Martin's in *South Pacific*.

Gordon Macrae, who starred on Broadway in *I Do! I Do!*, says he knew he wanted to be in show business since he was four years old.

"I was in the kindergarten orchestra," Mr. Macrae reminisces, "and I was a boy soprano. I acted in all the grammar school and high school plays and when I graduated from Deerfield Academy in 1940, I went out to the New York World's Fair and won a contest as a singer—first prize—a two weeks' singing engagement at fifty dollars a week with Les Brown's and Harry James's orchestras on Mike Todd's Dancing Campus. That was really the first money I earned as a performer.

"When that engagement was over, I heard about an opening at the Millpond Playhouse at Roslyn, Long Island, and I got the job. I think I clinched it because I owned a car and they needed transportation. I acted in a show called *The Trojan Horse* written by Christopher Morley. That didn't last long. I then got a job as a page boy at N.B.C. While there, I met a member of Horace Heidt's orchestra and auditioned for him, and became a singer in a choral group which led to my becoming a soloist with the orchestra.

"All during this time I kept studying music and taking dramatic lessons. When I left Horace Heidt's orchestra, my first job on Broadway as an actor was in *Junior Miss*. In the meantime I auditioned for Ray Block who was the orchestra leader on Ed Sullivan's radio show on which I appeared, but I guess my big break came one Sunday when Frank Sinatra got sick and I took his place on Sinatra's radio show. Some of the network brass heard me, and I was signed to a long-term contract with C.B.S.

"In order to get into the theatre, I advise young actors to study and perfect themselves in their particular gift. You must

The singer-actors of the off-Broadway musical, *Jacques
Brel Is Alive and Well and Living in Paris*, receiving
a backstage visit from the world-famous mime, Marcel
Marceau. *Left to right:* Elly Stone; Mort Shuman *(standing);*
Mini Yakim, director; Marcel Marceau; Alice Whitfield;
Shawn Elliott. *(Drake Studios)*

start from the bottom and learn as you go along. But I most emphatically urge actors to get a college degree. During the summers they can get theatrical experience in stock, the tent theatres, etc. More and more a college education is required of the actor as a background. In colleges offering acting courses and in campus theatres, the aspiring actor really gets his best opportunity to show what he can do."

11. Special Theatre Opportunities

There are many outlets today for trained dancers and singers. Although most performers set their sights on Broadway, they can find lucrative work in other forms of musical theatre.

One of the most important of these is the "industrial theatre" which has had a phenomenal growth since the early 50s when some inspired public relations man had the idea of hiring professionals to put on a show for his convention.

The actors audition exactly as they do for Broadway musical theatre, but the pay is far above Equity rates. Some of the shows run for two or three weeks, and all the available talent vies to get into these—even singers and dancers who are already employed—because industrial shows usually are put on in the morning and so the performers can still be in a Broadway production, and build up a tidy bank balance against the inevitable rainy day.

The Milliken Show (put on by the famous fabric house) is one of the best known, and the Oldsmobile Show, during its recent run, attracted some of the top talent on Broadway. DuPont, General Electric (which takes its shows on tour for as long as three months), Chevrolet, and other automobile and tire manufacturers also have shows.

Miss Dania Krupska directs, stages, and choreographs many of these important "industrials." She sends out a call to agents, Equity, etc., holds auditions, and is always on the lookout for a new talent.

The shows are given as a rule in the ballrooms of prominent hotels. The Milliken Show is usually staged in the big ballroom of the Waldorf and is attended by the executives of all the important dress houses that use Milliken fabrics, by important designers, buyers from all over the country, and by talent scouts and directors of shows for other big companies looking for talent.

The industrial musicals presented are usually condensations of current Broadway hits. Skilled writers and lyricists are engaged to tailor the words to fit the industrial product and to create company parodies of the original lyrics. The shows are superbly staged and mounted and the talent is well rehearsed. The production in every way resembles a Broadway musical.

Miss Krupska auditions talent and maintains an office at 564 West 52nd Street, New York 10019.

Night Clubs

Night clubs have always been a steppingstone to Broadway and offered a chance for new talent to find its way into the musical theatre. Most night club performers, even the big stars, would rather work in a Broadway show. They often use the New York clubs to show their talents, to keep their names before the public, and to earn money while waiting for a show. Carol Channing took to the night clubs during an arid stretch in her Broadway career after *Gentlemen Prefer Blondes,* and now that she is finished with *Hello, Dolly!,* Carol is again in the clubs, being paid a fortune.

Dancers and singers for the ensemble in a club show are auditioned in the same way as for musical theatre. Whether it is for Las Vegas, Florida, Chicago, or elsewhere, a call is sent out to the agents, Equity, *Variety, Show Business,* etc., for performers. They are auditioned and chosen for their talent, their skill, and their looks, but looks without talent is not enough these days; the chorus line even in a club show must know how to walk, sing, and, above all, dance.

Dinner Theatre

Still another source of employment for trained musical theatre talent is the "dinner theatre." These have sprung up all over the country and there are several around New York. One of them, the Meadowbrook Dinner Theatre, is in Cedar Grove, New Jersey, less than an hour from Broadway; the Wedgewood Dinner Theatre at Glen Cove, Long Island, also is close by.

For about seven dollars a patron has dinner and sees a musical. The shows are usually "standards" which are cut down to about an hour and a quarter of running time, and they are invariably built around a "name" performer (except in the boondocks where they'll take anyone who can give a creditable performance). The "name" performer, of course, gets the big money and the others are paid little more than the Equity minimum, but because of this, they offer a fertile field for new talent, and I have known many seasoned players who started in these places.

12. Ballet

The most dedicated people in the theatre are the ballet dancers. They seem to live in a world of their own, centered completely around the dance and the use of their own bodies in the dance. Many of them work at least twelve hours a day—at the barre, in rehearsal, and in performances.

I have watched a ballet dancer practice a physically demanding movement over and over again, stop for a while and practice another intricate step with accent on her other leg, return to the first step, and then just when it looked about perfect to me, stop with a despairing gesture, and "I'll never get the damn thing right," to prance off and start something new.

Ballet dancers have little interest in anything but the dance; they seldom go to a straight play and they see only musicals which feature unusual dancing; they eat, drink, and play among themselves and prefer to marry other dancers.

Some time ago when the late Walter Wanger, the film producer, had the idea of doing the now-famous *Cleopatra*, his original plan called for a low-budget but beautiful film without a high-priced star. He asked if I could recommend a talented young girl with an exceptionally exquisite body, and I immediately thought of one of the top ballerinas in City Center's New York City Ballet.

I sent Walter her photographs and he was enchanted with them and asked to meet her. We came together at luncheon and Walter explained the story to her, the shooting schedule, and the fact that he would like to do some of the filming on location in Egypt.

The beautiful ballerina continued her luncheon of steak and salad (the dancers' usual menu) noncommittally. Finally Walter came to the point of saying he would like to arrange a screen test for her and because the ballet company was in the midst of its New York season, he said he would bring his cameraman on from California for her convenience.

It was only then that she looked up and said casually, "But, Mr. Wanger, I am a ballet dancer. I have no desire to be a film actress."

I often think how different the history not only of *Cleopatra* but of Elizabeth Taylor and Richard Burton would have been had Allegra Kent not been a dedicated ballerina.

Ballet History

Catherine de Medici is credited with bringing the ballet to France from her native Italy when she became the bride of the Duc d'Orléans. She commissioned her Italian Intendant of Music, Baltazarini, whom she later gave the French name of Beaujoyeulx, to invent a *divertissement,* which is considered by historians to have been "the first, modern, integrated theatrical dance drama."

Beaujoyeulx called his entertainment the Ballet Comique de la Reine—a fusion of poetry, music, and dance. For some two hundred and fifty years France was the home of ballet and its center of development.

The rules laid down in France spread throughout Europe as French-trained dancers became teachers in Denmark, Sweden, Italy, Germany, Austria, England, Spain, and Russia.

The French Revolution rid the ballet of cumbersome hoop-skirted costumes; a new freedom was found in light dresses modeled on the classic tunics and robes of ancient Greece.

High-heeled shoes were replaced by the classic flat dancing slippers tied with laces in the manner of sandals.

Ballet entered a period of decline in Western Europe during the Victorian era, but in 1907 it was revivified in Russia by Sergei Diaghilev, and in 1909 he organized the great Ballet Russe and was associated with the legendary Nijinsky, Pavlova, Massine, Fokine, and Stravinsky. His schools trained dancers whose traditions are still carried on to the present day.

Michel Fokine, one of Russia's famous teachers and ballet masters, instituted further costume reforms and his ballets were models of construction. He came to America in 1918 and lived and worked here until his death in 1942. He influenced and freed today's choreographers from the rigidity of the past for the fluidity and creativity of the present.

Ballet Today

"Balanchine's best work is in pure ballet. Lucia Chase has built the most splendid ballet company in this country. What I did," says Agnes de Mille, "was introduce a very clear and simple form of ballet to great numbers of people. Most people had seen only bad ballet so that *Oklahoma!*, *One Touch of Venus*, *Carousel*, and *Brigadoon* gave them their first exposure to good ballet. By the time they got out of the theatre, they were interested in it."

Miss de Mille says five million young girls in this country are studying to be professional dancers. Only a very small percentage of them will ever reach the stage—any stage. As they progress from childhood to young womanhood, their own limitations will become evident to them. Health, strength, endurance, body proportions (long legs are important and an absolute necessity in George Balanchine's New York City Ballet), and above all the talent or gift that will make this most demanding career one's important goal are requisites.

Some will fall by the wayside because of a lack of available advanced dancing schools—although there are good schools in almost every important city—or lack of funds to continue. Then, too, many families will push these girls into what they consider more secure work, and there is always the prospect of early marriage. But for those who do persevere, and find the necessary training, there are always ways and means.

Melissa Hayden, ballerina of the New York City (Center) Ballet, had a rather late start as a dancer. "I was about twelve and a half years old," she told me. "I had a friend who was studying dancing, and one day I went to the studio with her. I thought I'd like to learn to dance, too, so I convinced my mother that I should take lessons.

"My home is in Toronto and I was fortunate enough to go to the Boris Volkoff School of Ballet. I studied there about two years, not too seriously, and then I saw the original Ballet Russe which was on tour, and I was hooked! I decided then and there to become a ballerina."

Miss Hayden, as if to make up for lost time, began to work with all her heart, taking as many classes as she was allowed. To help pay for them, she had a series of jobs—she learned bookkeeping at one point—and she saved enough money at the same time to come to New York.

Her first engagement was at the Radio City Music Hall in the corps de ballet, and in between the four shows a day, she managed to take two classes at the Vilzah-Shollar School and the Ballet Arts School where she studied Italian and Russian ballet.

"Also at the Vilzah school," Miss Hayden recalls, "Michael Kidd was taking dancing lessons. There were many dancers from the ballet studying there. Mr. Kidd sent me to Ballet Theatre, and I was interviewed by the company manager who said they had already completed auditions for the season, but he took my name and address and said he would call me.

"I went home rather downhearted, but a short time later I had a call from the Ballet Russe. Although New York is a big city, the ballet world is small, and the following day, evidently having learned the Ballet Russe was interested in me, the Ballet Theatre called me back. So I had not one but two chances at the same time!"

Miss Hayden remained with Ballet Theatre for two and a half years and with them toured London and the Continent. She also traveled across the United States, sometimes playing one-night stands in the smaller cities, but always studying and perfecting her craft and gaining tremendous skill.

When George Balanchine and Lincoln Kirstein founded the City Center's New York City Ballet in 1949, they invited Miss Hayden to join. She is one of the company's official charter members.

On the other hand, Edward Villella, also a star of the New York City Ballet, started as a ballet dancer—and purely by accident.

"I had a sister who was studying dancing at the Ann Garrison School in Bayside, Long Island, where we lived," he told me. "My mother took her to her lessons, leaving me to play with my little friends. One day in a rough game I was knocked unconscious, and that was how she found me when she came home. After that my mother never left me alone and took me along when my sister went for her lessons.

"I was ten years old at the time. To keep me occupied, Miss Garrison suggested I take lessons, too. At first I didn't want to, but finally I took a lesson and found I loved it. A little later, my sister auditioned for the School of American Ballet and they accepted her. My mother happened to mention that she had a son who took dancing lessons, too.

"When they heard 'boy dancer,' they were eager to have a look at me. I took a class with them and they gave me a scholarship."

Recalling his first public appearance, Mr. Villella said it

was in Bayside. "The family had a friend, a music teacher, who gave recitals for her pupils, and she invited my sister and me to dance."

Mr. Villella's first professional dancing appearance was in an off-Broadway show called *Living Life* at the Phoenix Theatre in New York. It lasted only a week, but it led to his being invited to join the New York City Ballet in December, 1957.

Military duty interrupted Mr. Villella's career. He joined the New York State Maritime College and was in the Naval Reserve for four years during which time he didn't dance at all. It was difficult to get back after this, but hard work and perseverance did it and at this writing, he is at the very top of a very great career.

Mr. Villella did a full-length film of *Nutcracker* in Munich which was shown twice on television in this country and he also completed a film of Balanchine's production of "Midsummer Night's Dream" in which he is Oberon.

He was seen by millions in the television "special" of *Brigadoon* playing the roll of Harry Beaton which he did first for me in City Center productions of this beautiful musical. He is not only a superb dancer but a fine actor and an excellent choreographer.

Ballet Opportunities

In my lifetime I have seen ballet grow from a special performing art form relished by a comparatively small band of wildly enthusiastic balletomanes to virtually world-size popularity. There are often two major ballet companies playing to packed houses in Lincoln Center. The Royal Ballet will be at the Metropolitan Opera House with Rudolf Nureyev and Margot Fonteyn enthralling staid businessmen who wouldn't have been caught dead at performances a few years ago, and just across the beautiful Lincoln Center Plaza at City Center's State Theatre, our New York City Ballet or Lucia Chase's magnificent American Ballet Theatre (so-called because this company specailizes in "story" or theatre ballets) also is selling out.

The recently adopted City Center Joffrey Ballet comes close to selling out at their home on Fifty-fifth Street, and when it presents "Astarte" or "The Clowns," you cannot buy a ticket.

Another major company—the Rebekah Harkness Foundation Ballet, called Harkness Ballet, Inc.—is growing in importance and has its own followers.

Unfortunately the good old Ballet Russe de Monte Carlo, the original resident company at City Center years ago, has been disbanded. Sergei Denham, who piloted it through so many difficult years, deserves more than a word of credit for his indefatigable pioneering spirit in those days when ballet was for the very few, and even wonderful Fiorello LaGuardia remarked of its coming to City Center, "I hope you know what you're doing. I personally would never go to see a bunch of guys in tights jumping around and making fools of themselves."

There are less well-known but excellent ballet companies in many cities outside of New York and there is a never-ending need for young dancers, for the average ballet dancer's career is a short one and the ranks must be kept filled with new and younger talent each season.

Auditions are held regularly by all the companies and if you want to make this exacting craft your career, do not hesitate to apply. You will be greeted with open arms and be inaugurated into a most select and special family if you have the training and, of course, the talent.

Part Three: Behind the Footlights

13. The Stage Manager

Backstage the production stage manager is the boss. He is also the producer's right hand. So I will begin the look at backstage life with him.

Once the producer decides on the play and has engaged the director and the scenic designer, the stage manager is present at most of their conferences. After several meetings and a careful analysis of the script, the stage manager confers with the property man about the furniture and properties needed for the period and setting of the play.

He also must have a clear picture of the director's interpretation of the action and the mood of the play, and his ideas about character development. If the stage designer is going to do his own lighting, the stage manager must talk with him about the kinds of lamps and the number of them necessary. He also attends all interviews and auditions for the casting of the play.

The stage manager notifies the actors when rehearsals are to begin, and at the first rehearsal he reads extracts from the Actors' Equity contract to the assembled cast to make certain they understand their responsibilities and the responsibilities of "management."

He has received floor plans from the scenic designer and he has marked out the floor of the rehearsal hall or stage with colored tape so the actors will know the boundaries and areas. He also has arranged to have substitute furniture—usually chairs, benches, and tables—on hand when the rehearsals start.

He attends every rehearsal, sitting with the director and his assistants; he keeps in touch with the costume designer and costume maker and arranges for appointments with the actors for their fittings. He posts all notices pertaining to any changes in time or location of rehearsals and makes sure the actors are kept informed.

When the settings are put up on the stage, the work is done under the supervision of the designer, the carpenter, and the stage manager. The furniture is placed and marked and dress rehearsals start.

If the play has many scenes, it is the stage manager who, with the designer, works out the schemes for the most effective and quickest changes; the stage manager's is the last word in definite instructions to the stagehands.

The stage manager assigns dressing rooms for the players in accordance with the order of billing, already worked out by the producer and the press agent. This often takes a great deal of diplomacy because every actor is a star in his own estimation.

Before each performance the stage manager makes the "calls" for the performers; he calls—usually via a speaker system into the dressing rooms—the half hour, fifteen minutes, and the final "on stage" before the curtain rises. It is his responsibility to make sure that the actors are on stage on time.

After the play opens, the stage manager must make sure that the actors continue to perform their roles exactly as the director rehearsed them. If any of them deviate from the original direction, it is the stage manager's responsibility to correct them and sometimes it is even necessary for him to call a complete rehearsal, if performances have gone really haywire.

Rehearsals for Understudies

The stage manager calls frequent rehearsals for the understudies because it is his responsibility to be sure the understudy is ready to take over on short notice. Since the understudy is seldom given any original instructions by the director of the play, the stage manager has an opportunity to use his ability as a director at these rehearsals, even though he is only re-creating the original work. Many good directors have made their start as stage managers: Hal Prince, George Abbott, Herman Shumlin, Alfred de Liagre, Milton Katselas and many others.

The stage manager also must see that the understudies have the proper costumes, that the costumes fit perfectly and are exactly like the originals. When the costumes are extremely expensive, some producers pick understudies the same size as the principals in order to avoid the necessity of buying a double set.

All costumes must be kept clean and in repair, and while this is the work of the wardrobe department, it is the stage manager who checks and makes sure. The scenery is given a thorough inspection by the stage manager at least once a week. In the case of a long run it is sometimes necessary for him to order painters in for retouching.

Though the props are, of course, the special problem of the property man, the stage manager must inspect them weekly too. In fact, the stage manager must check all departments—property, carpentry, lighting, wardrobe, and sound, if it is used—before every performance.

Getting the props can turn out to be an all-inclusive effort, especially when an authentic period atmosphere is essential: the producer, the director, the stage manager, the author, and members of the cast often lend or sell articles from their homes that will create that atmosphere.

When we did *Life With Father* at City Center, Mrs. Clarence Day, whose husband wrote the book from which the play was fashioned, let us use several family portraits, and Dorothy Stickney, who re-created her original role of "Mother" for us, let us use several of her chairs.

Some property men—veritable geniuses—know just where to

Property List

All furniture and props must be of the 1880's period.

ON STAGE

1 Tabouret!e
   1 vase of flowers
   2 books
1 silver topped glass jar (for
   cigars)
   Cigars
   Match stand
   Old fashioned Parlor matches
1 Arm chair
1 Stand
1 Jardiniere
1 Rubber plant
2 Stands
2 Jardinieres
2 Palms
2 Side tables or console tables,
   with drawers
2 Large Vases
4 Smaller vases
2 Brass framed photographs
1 Set fire irons
1 Set andirons
1 Bronze clock
2 Urns with plumes
2 Chandelabras
1 what-not stand and ornaments
   (about 12 pieces)
1 Small armchair
1 End table
   Vase of flowers
   3 books
   1 Figurette
1 Sofa
1 Cushion
1 Occasional table
   1 Lamp
   1 Large ornament
   2 Framed photographs
1 Extension table—6'x 4'
4 Small chairs
2 Armchairs
1 Stool
Drapes for window and door in hallway
Lace curtains for window
Lambrican for mantel-piece
6 Drinking glasses— for milk
18 Service plates
12 smaller plates
12 glass plates for fruit
12 glass castors for fruit
6 cereal bowls
18 Coffee cups and saucers
12 Butter pats
12 Knives
12 forks

12 teaspoons
6 fruit spoons
1 Silver toast rack
4 silver salt and pepper shakers
1 serving spoon
1 serving fork
6 silver napkin rings
4 platters
1 silver coffee pot
1 silver creamer
1 silver sugar bowl
1 silver sugar spoon
3 medium sized glass plates for cakes
2 large black trays
1 large fancy tray
1 large silver tray
1 small silver tray
1 silver salver
1 small round tray
1 silver teapot
1 silver tea-set sugar bowl
12 tea cups and saucers
6 small tea spoons
4 breakfast table cloths
   12 tea napkins
24 breakfast napkins

The above list of tableware includes coverage for breakage etc.

FOR OFF STAGE USE

2 large silencers for breakfast table
1 False table-top
Copy of New York Times— 1888
Copy of New York Evening Sun—1888
Copy of Youth's Companion—1888
1 Old fashioned doorbell on springs
1 Postman's whistle
1 Stereoscope +Picture
Several pictures for same
Supply of writing paper and envelopes
   Blue-Pink-Lavender-white
   White business envelopes
   Pencils
Stage money
6 coins-half dollar
1 handsome leather wallet-for Father
1 coin purse— for Father
Crash effect of ANNIE falling downstairs
   tin tray
   Broken dishes and boxes
   1 padded stick-for falling body
Brown wrapping paper(for medicine boxes)
Blue wrapping paper(for pug-dog and suitcases)
Ball of white string
Ball of heavy twine
1 box of Tiddlewinks
1 Sheet music "The Merry Farmer"
1 Piano—Offstage

Property list for *Life With Father*.

24 household bills of different sizes and colors
1 handsome household account book
Newspaper clipping-for JOHN
2 shoe boxes-to be wrapped for
  BOX LUNCH
Supply of boxes for medicine-each
  supposed to hold 2 dozen 8ounce bottles
2 eight ounce old fashioned medicine bottles
Labels for same-as per SCRIPT
1 Copper tea kettle
2 hand towels
1 Doctor's satchel
1 china pug dog
Box for china dog
Supply of tissue paper
3 yards of red ribbon-1½ inch wide-
  Cut in two pieces-one piece mussed,
  one piece ironed
1 Jewelers' ring box
1 ring-must be very handsome
1 suit box
Label for same
1 Purse-For VINNIE
1 Fancy table cloth
2 Ladies traveling bags-of 1880
1 Handsome white prayer book-For VINNIE
1 Small black prayer book for Dr. Lloyd
2 Cames-for Father
1 Watch and chain, cigar cutter for FATHER
Eye-glasses and ribbon-for FATHER
1 piece of petit point in hoops-for VINNIE
Yarn, needle and thimble-for VINNIE
1 Bowl for center of table
Supply of artificial fruit for same
1 Flower frog for same
Cigars
Matches (Old-fashioned Parlor matches)
2 Bonnet boxes
1 Shirt-waist box
1 Corset box
5 different size packages
Roll of bandage
Roll of adhesive tape-both these for HARLAN

                    PERISHABLES

Bananas-(to fry and use for kippers)
oranges
Bacon
Canned apricots(These used for scrambled eggs)
Coffee
Tea
Bread
Cake-(Brown and white cakes)
Milk
Sugar
Rice crispies (for oatmeal)
Bottle of burnt sugar for Patent medicine
Biscuits
Ladyfinger cake

Cup cake
1 sm. of cinnamon (to be used on fried bananas)
Butter

NOTE FOR PROPERTY MAN:

In order to get the best effect of using apricots for scrambled
eggs, we used a number of pieces of toast, cut in squares of
about two and a half inches and made a three-tier pyramid of
these in the center of platter and put apricots on top of toast.
The bacon was then put around the edge of the platter.

In Act III., Scene 1, use fake kippers on platter on table,
and one half of a fried banana on plates of Father and elder
boys for eating.

NOTE TO PROPERTY MAN:

The quick changes to and from the breakfast scenes, were made
by having a false table top, the same size as the extended
table, already set, off Right, and carried on by two men and
put on table R.C.

The window on the right wall was in a separate flat, hinged to
the next flat upstage. This can be opened during the changes
and the fake table top carried on or off through this opening.

turn to find unusual articles, or concoct them themselves. And food for the stage takes special concocting. For the scenes at the breakfast table, our City Center property man, Edward Conley, fashioned fried eggs from rounds of white bread with half a tinned apricot for the yoke. The dumplings Pearl Bailey devours in *Hello, Dolly!* are fashioned by St. James Theatre property man, Leo Herbert, of spun sugar—cotton candy.

If the curtain is supposed to go up at eight thirty, the stage manager is the one who gives the order to take it up. Sometimes when there is heavy rain, or there is a theatre party and the audience is coming in slowly, the house manager asks the stage manager to hold the curtain for a few minutes—usually not more than ten.

Calling the Cues

In order to carry out his many, all-important tasks, the stage manager has one or two assistants on whom he can absolutely rely. For straight plays, as a rule, he has one assistant; for musicals he has two.

It has become the custom to have the first assistant stage manager "on the book"—to call the cues—during rehearsals. This gives the production stage manager the freedom to check all the other details of the performance. He is very fortunate if he can choose his own assistant but frequently the director brings in someone with whom he has worked and whom he likes to have on the book. In this case, the first assistant is also more or less an assistant to the director.

The assistant stage manager who has been on the book is the one who actually runs the show during performances. He has the highly concentrated work of calling all the cues for lights, sound, curtain, etc. In musicals, "travelers" are often used between scenes; they open and close with considerable frequency. A "traveler" is a curtain, so-called because it travels across the stage and is not dropped down from above.

There are often more than a hundred cues to be given during the performance of a musical, and the smooth running of the show depends enormously on the timing and ability of the stage manager on the book.

Qualifications

A strong nervous system and a highly developed sense of diplomacy are absolute requisites for a superior stage manager. He must be the one who keeps calm no matter how stormy a situation becomes and who soothes when temperaments clash—as they sometimes do. He must cope with emergencies, no matter how harrowing—from suddenly having to replace a player to ringing down the curtain in case of utter disaster. His main thought always is "the show must go on" if humanly possible, and he must find ways to cover up blunders and to do so so skillfully that the audience will not realize that something went wrong.

When the play he is working on becomes a success, the stage manager prepares the script for publication, including all of the director's notes (stage business, etc.), so that stock and amateur companies can reproduce the play with approximately the same staging.

A Success Story

Herman Shapiro, who has been my production stage manager on Broadway and at the New York City Center for twenty years, says: "My many years of acting taught me the things that qualified me as a stage manager. I was virtually born in the theatre. A great many members of my family were theatre people and it was just natural for me to go into one of their plays when there was an opening for a young actor.

"After several years on the stage, I decided I didn't have sufficient education and while I was working with Moss Hart

ROSA. You can't think of a lie?

SERAFINA. He was a—truckdriver, cara. He got in a fight, he was chase by—policemen!

ROSA. They chased him into your bedroom?

SERAFINA. I took pity on him, I give him first aid, I let him sleep on the floor. He give me his promise—he . . .

ROSA. Did he kneel in front of Our Lady? Did he promise that he would respect your innocence?

SERAFINA. Oh, cara, cara! (*Abandoning all pretense.*) He was Sicilian; he had rose oil in his hair and the rose tattoo of your father. In the dark room I couldn't see his clown face. I closed my eyes and dreamed that he was your father! I closed my eyes! I dreamed that he was your father. . . .

ROSA. Basta, basta, non voglio sentire più niente! The only thing worse than a liar is a liar that's also a hypocrite!

SERAFINA. Senti, per favore! (*Rosa wheels about from the mirror and fixes her mother with a long and withering stare. Serafina cringes before it.*) Don't look at me like that with the eyes of your father! (*She shields her face as from a terrible glare.*)

ROSA. Yes, I am looking at you with the eyes of my father. I see you the way he saw you. (*She runs to the table and seizes the piggy bank.*) Like this, this pig! (*Serafina utters a long, shuddering cry like a cry of childbirth.*) I need five dollars. I'll take it out of this! (*Rosa smashes the piggy bank to the floor and rakes some coins into her purse. Serafina stoops to the floor. There is the sound of a train whistle. Rosa is now fully dressed, but she hesitates, a little ashamed of her cruelty—but only a little. Serafina cannot meet her daughter's eyes. At last the girl speaks.*)

SERAFINA. How beautiful—is my daughter! Go to the boy!

ROSA. (*As if she might be about to apologize.*) Mama? He didn't touch me—he just said—"Che bella!" (*Serafina turns slowly, shamefully, to face her. She is like a peasant in the presence of a young princess. Rosa stares at her a moment longer, then suddenly catches her breath and runs out of the house. As the girl leaves, Serafina calls:*)

SERAFINA. Rosa, Rosa, the—wrist watch! (*Serafina snatches up the little gift box and runs out onto the porch with it. She starts to call her daughter again, holding the gift out toward her, but her*

86

City Center stage manager Herman Shapiro's method for marking cues in scripts: "My method is to mark WARNINGS in red at the side of the script. Either side will do. I mark the cue in blue at the word or action. I call the warning well ahead. For example WARNING LITE CUE 65—and about a line ahead of the actual cue I repeat LITE 65—and on the cue GO. Arrangements can be made with the electrician as to how the calls will be made."

and Dore Schary as an actor at night, I attended law school at Rutgers, New Jersey, in the afternoons. I received my law degree and was admitted to the bar in New Jersey even though I had no intention of ever practicing law. Many of the young men I knew who were anxious to pass the bar examination and practice law failed. I really believe I sailed through because it didn't mean that much to me and I was not at all tense about it.

"I continued as an actor for several years and worked in Walter Huston's company for two seasons. My first job as a stage manager was with Jed Harris. I had been with him for many years when Jed directed *Red Gloves* with Charles Boyer for Jean Dalrymple and he brought me to her. I have been with her ever since.

"Besides my work as production stage manager at City Center, I am also in charge of City Center's huge warehouse where their drama and musical scenery and properties are stored. It is a huge five-story building, jammed full. I fortunately know where everything is and how I can get at it and, when we are going to do a certain play or musical, it is up to me to take two or three stagehands to the warehouse and dig out the entire production, down to the last smallest hand prop.

"I also arrange with the trucking firm for transporting all this to City Center. The hours for taking the scenery in and out are arranged by me with split-second timing. At City Center, one show immediately follows another and the sets must be removed the moment one production ends. The sets for the new show then must be brought in and all this, if possible, must be accomplished during daily working hours or we would run into the superexpensive overtime. Even during the day there are what are known as 'golden hours' which are paid for double because the truckmen should be at luncheon or dinner at these times. It is pretty difficult and takes the utmost ingenuity to figure out how to get the old scenery out and the new scenery in without running into these 'golden hours' of overtime."

Of course today a young man who would like to become a stage manager can learn the craft not only in the professional theater as an actor or as an assistant but through study at a university. There is no limit to the time one must give to learning the tricks of the trade in stage management, and the more one has absorbed, the better stage manager he will be.

14. The Producer

Today money appears to be the important requisite for a theatrical producer—the producer's own money or money he is able to raise. Since a producer receives no income from a play until it is in production, and then very little until all costs are paid and a profit is made (which he shares fifty-fifty with his financial backers), it is pretty obvious that today's theatrical producer must have some other source of income.

Fortunately for the theatre, all kinds of talented people become dedicated to getting a play or musical going. It is surprising how disparate the backgrounds of the present Broadway producers are.

David Merrick is indisputably Broadway's reigning king. Both his successes and his failures are spectacular, but his hits far outnumber his flops—to use the Broadway vernacular.

David Merrick arrived in New York from St. Louis where he had been on the brink of becoming a very successful lawyer when he was overtaken by an inexplicable and powerful urge to become a theatrical producer. He set about to fulfill his new ambition methodically, first studying show business from every angle, especially the financial and business management ends.

He came to New York well-fortified by savings and spent a year or two continuing his studies in and about the theatre while he waited for what he considered a fairly foolproof presentation. It turned out to be *Fanny* and his partner-stage director was Joshua Logan, fresh from a series of triumphs including the great *South Pacific*. *Fanny's* music was by Harold Rome; the book was by S. N. Behrman, based on a series of stories by Marcel Pagnol called *Marius, Fanny and César*. The stars were Ezio Pinza, Walter Slezak, and Florence Henderson.

On paper it looked foolproof enough; and for my taste it was a delightfully entertaining, amusing, and touching musical, but the critics felt otherwise. The "mixed notices" didn't phase David Merrick. His exploitation was magnificent and before long he had *Fanny* propelled into a success and a long, lucrative run.

The rest is Broadway history. Mr. Merrick has had, by his own count, fifty-five hits which include *Look Back in Anger, The World of Susie Wong, Gypsy, A Taste of Honey, Becket,* and currently *Forty Carats* and *Promises, Promises*. In one season he had six hits running on Broadway: *Cactus Flower, I Do! I Do!, Don't Drink the Water, Rosencrantz and Guildenstern Are Dead, How Now, Dow Jones* and the perennial *Hello, Dolly!*

Harold Prince hasn't done as many shows as David Merrick, but he has a spectacular percentage of hits. He started as a stage manager for George Abbott and developed into Mr. Abbott's partner in the production of *The Pajama Game*. He was very young at that time and very firm about his likes and dislikes—so much so that the author of the book, originally called *7½ Cents,* later wrote an amusing play called *Say, Darling* about his experiences with the freshman producer.

Prince was known as Broadway's *Wunderkind* for a long time and his success was attributed to Lady Luck. The fact that he is enormously gifted and a fastidious worker was overlooked until he had proved himself over and over, not only as a producer but as an inventive and sensitive director.

The magnificent *Fiddler on the Roof*, which he produced, and the bittersweet *Cabaret* which he produced and directed,

Harold Prince (with worry beads), Harold Hastings (musical director), and John Kander (composer) during a rehearsal of *Zorba'*, produced and directed by Mr. Prince. *(Friedman-Abeles)*

are only two of his long-running international successes. And his new musical, *Zorba'*, is already a hit.

Saint Subber hadn't had a production on Broadway for many years—not since his *The Grass Harp*, the play by Truman Capote which was a succès d'estime, with only a moderate run. Then he "discovered" playwright Neil Simon whose first play, the hilarious *Come Blow Your Horn*, had been dismissed by the critics, but had been taken to its heart by a fun-loving public.

Mr. Simon had had his second comedy tried out at the summer theatre in Bucks County, Pennsylvania, where again it was sloughed off by critics as unimportant writing and judged by know-all theatre people, including several vaguely interested producers, to have irremediable "third-act trouble." But Saint Subber was not among them. With unerring instinct he engaged an unknown director, Mike Nichols, and a cast of delightful comedians and turned Neil Simon's "unimportant little comedy" into the long-running *Barefoot in the Park*. He followed this with two more of Mr. Simon's successes, *The Odd Couple* and *Plaza Suite*, both directed by Mike Nichols.

Saint Subber has been around Broadway all his life, for his parents ran a popular theatre ticket agency in Times Square. He first went to work in the theatre as an assistant to director-producer John Murray Anderson and worked up to being his stage manager before taking the plunge with his own production of *Out of This World*.

Alexander N. Cohen ties David Merrick for showmanship. His after-theatre parties are legendary in the amount of publicity they garner. After one opening in the early fall, he took over Shubert Alley (the private lane that runs between 44th and 45th Streets, past the stage doors of the Booth and Shubert theatres) and gave a sort of private block party for his cast, celebrities, and the press. He was director of publicity of the Bulova Watch Company for many years, and held onto that highly paid position while he produced several plays. Finally he had a number of important successes, including *At the Drop of a Hat, An Evening with Mike Nichols and Elaine May, An Evening with Yves Montand, Beyond the Fringe,* Lena Horne's *Nine O'Clock Review,* and *An Evening with Maurice Chevalier,* all of which made him large sums of money. He has since devoted his entire time to Broadway productions, including the Richard Burton *Hamlet* and the beautiful *The School for Scandal* which he imported *in toto* from London.

Importing a Play

Importing a ready-made hit from London seems an easy way of becoming a producer, but actually it is not as foolproof as one would imagine. There have been many plays which have enjoyed great success and long runs in London—such as *The Severed Head, The Right Honorable Gentlemen,* and *The Chinese Prime Minister*—which were failures on Broadway.

This is not always due to a difference in our tastes. Sometimes it is because of the difficulty of recasting. The Actors' Equity Association now has a most complicated ruling on the use of alien actors.

In order for the producer to use the original London star or stars, he now must first present an application, script, and other pertinent material to the League of New York Theatres.

A representative appointed by the League will consider the application. If the representative does not support the application, the producer is notified that his request is denied.

If the League representative supports the application, the producer must submit the script and pertinent material to Equity.

Within one week after the receipt of the application, the producer will be notified whether Equity approves or has an objection. If Equity objects, the Equity and League representatives will meet. If they agree, their decision will be binding on both Equity and the producer.

If Equity and the League of New York Theatres disagree, then not later than one week after their meeting another meeting will be held with an impartial arbitrator (a list of arbitrators has been designated by the League and Equity). Not later than one week after that hearing, the arbitrator will hand down his decision, which is binding on both parties.

In arriving at his decision, the arbitrator will use as criteria the H-1 and H-2 definitions of an essential alien worker of the United States Immigration Service:

H-1. A star of unusual ability who is required in a specified role or play which demands his distinct merit and ability.

H-2. A top role for which there is no resident alien or American actor suitable.

These complicated rules do not apply when an entire company such as the Old Vic or the Royal Shakespeare is brought over for a tour by an impresario such as Sol Hurok, as long as the company presents two or more plays. In the case of a commercial West End-to-Broadway transferral, however, the above rules must be strictly adhered to.

The original London director can be brought in from London with no difficulty, even though directors are members of Equity. But very often the director will not come without most of the original cast.

Of course the reverse is true, too. American successes have come a cropper in London because British Actors' Equity has more or less the same rules, and there are some American plays which become ludicrous caricatures of themselves when played by a British cast.

The Equity rules apply not only to British actors but to all aliens. An actor I very much admire is the Mexican star, Manolo Fabregas, who produces, directs, and acts at his own Teatro Fabregas in Mexico City. The theatre was founded by his grandmother who was as famous in Latin America as Ethel Barrymore was here. When Manolo heard I was going to revive *The King and I* at City Center, he telephoned me from

Mexico and said he had always wanted to be seen as the King in New York as he had had great success playing it throughout Latin America. (Manolo speaks perfect English; he was educated in the United States.)

I was having great difficulty casting the part anyway, so I decided to have him play it. But what a time I had trying to convince Equity that he was a star! It was only after the President of Mexico, the American ambassador, and several other of Manolo's friends intervened that I was able to present him. He was a great success, by the way, and the wife of the President of Mexico made a special trip to New York to see his performance.

Starting a Production

The producer of an original play for Broadway generally starts with a script which has attracted him sufficiently to make him plunge ahead through the many steps necessary to bring the written word to the stage.

If he is creative (rather rare these days), he may start by giving the author suggestions for what he feels should be done to perfect the script. If he is creative and experienced, and not a complete egotist, he will first confer with the director he has selected; if the director agrees with him about the possibilities for success of the play, they will both confer with the author. If he is the more usual promoter-producer, he probably will leave the director and the author to work alone.

The producer then turns over to his general manager some of the chores the old-time producers did themselves. In fact, years ago they were called managers, not producers, and Actors' Equity still refers to them in all contracts as "the management." (Alfred de Liagre is one of the few present-day producers who still likes to do all "the management" himself.)

The first thing the general manager does is put up a bond with Equity. This is an amount of money equal to two weeks' salary for the entire cast. No actors may be signed before this bond is posted. In fact, Equity will not give a producer a set of contracts until the money is in its hands. The bond is recoverable at the end of the play's run.

Often the bond is put up from what is known as "front money," which is the producer's own cash or money he borrows until he has completely financed the play. Before all the money for the overall production budget has been raised, there are considerable preliminary expenses, including the advance royalty to the author due on the signing of the formal Dramatists' Guild contract. Hence the necessity for front money.

The producer and/or the general manager takes no further steps as a rule until there is a Broadway home for the play and perhaps two or three out-of-town theatres where tryout performances can be given. Each theatre must be bonded or guaranteed with a preliminary payment of from $6,000 to $13,500 a week for two weeks in New York, and the same amount per week for the entire engagement out of town. This is an advance against the theatre's percentage of the gross box-office receipts; the theatre often gets 35 percent and the production 65 percent.

New Haven, Boston, Philadelphia, Wilmington, and Detroit are the cities preferred for pre-Broadway work, and their theatres are usually kept busy throughout the entire season.

Everyone, down to the dresser for the star, is important to the overall production, and it is the producer's function to make sure that he has put together a combination of experts who will work together harmoniously. In fact, one of the most important things a producer has to do, after selecting the script and raising the money, is "keep the peace," for there will be dozens, sometimes scores, of personalities and temperaments to be dealt with, and dissension, unhappiness, turmoil, and friction among them must be avoided like the plague.

One troublemaker can be like the rotten apple, and it is

sometimes because of this—not because of lack of ability or talent—that sudden startling cast changes are announced in the newspapers. The backstage changes go unheralded.

After the staff is settled upon, and the stars or featured players are agreed upon, general auditions to fill the other roles begin.

When the actors have been engaged, the general manager or producer makes sure that all the Equity contracts are duly signed and the necessary "riders" attached. "Riders" spell out special conditions the actor insists upon:

His billing

The number of house seats he will be allotted for each performance: usually three pair, to take care of friends, relatives, agents, etc., who would have difficulty getting good seats at the box office if the show is a hit (house seats are paid for; they are not passes)

His dressing room: on stage, on first floor, "must have air conditioning," or "need refrigerator"

Private dresser and/or hairdresser

Special privileges: time off to do a film or television show

How his salary is to be paid: cash to him, check to his business manager

Geraldine Page, starring in my summer circuit production of *The Little Foxes*, had in her rider "transportation to be supplied for three children, two nursemaids, and one hairdresser."

The Company Manager

Sometimes the producer's general manager is also the company manager in which case he must be a member of ATPAM —The Association of Theatrical Press Agents and Managers. He becomes a full member of this craft union by serving as an apprentice with an accredited manager for a minimum period of sixty weeks (this can be spread over several seasons).

As company manager he has many responsibilities:

He must know the many rules and bylaws of the Actors' Equity Association and make sure that they are adhered to at all times by both the management and the actors.

He must know the rules and regulations of IATSE (International Alliance of Theatrical Stage Employees), the stagehands' union.

He must know the rules and working conditions of the American Federation of Musicians, Local 802, for Broadway shows.

He makes up the payroll for the entire company, making the proper deductions from their salaries for Federal withholding tax, state income tax, city withholding tax, FICA (Social Security), and disability insurance.

He makes up a payroll statement for the management showing the amounts to be paid to Equity for the Equity League Pension Trust Fund, unemployment, hospitalization, and disability.

He "counts up"—counts the number of tickets sold and checks that against unsold tickets to verify the box-office treasurer's statement of receipts for each performance.

If the star's salary includes a percentage of the gross, the company manager makes sure the star receives a copy of the statement.

He pays royalties to author, director, choreographer, and others according to contracts.

He pays all bills pertaining to the production as they accrue including: insurance, accountant, and legal fees.

He must be familiar with the theatre's contract and know which part of expenses the house (theatre) pays: what part of the stagehands' bill, the musicians' bill, and the advertising.

He prepares a weekly statement for the producer showing profit or loss.

It is the company manager who has the closest contact with the actors once the play has opened, and a pleasant, diplomatic manager can do a great deal to keep the company happy, especially during a tour or the out-of-town tryout period.

He buys all the tickets and makes all arrangements for travel; he arranges for the hauling of the scenery, and he knows how much time the stagehands will need to take down the sets and load them.

He travels with the company and with the help of the stage manager sees that the actors are on time for transportation calls, photography calls, etc. Upon arrival of the troupe out-of-town, he makes sure everyone has a place to live and has received his baggage; he recommends places to eat and generally acts as a good shepherd.

Another important member of the producer's staff is the press representative. In the case of a first production, the press agent is usually someone with a valuable reputation whose name will be included in the prospectus as a part of the optimistic picture.

Production Costs

The cost of Broadway theatre producing is fantastic. It seems incredible but scenery—painted canvas and unfinished lumber—can cost more than a modest suburban house with two baths, finished basement, appliances, two-car garage, on a nice plot of land, tastefully landscaped.

To give you some idea where the money goes, the following is a minimum production budget for a one-set, five-character, straight play:

Scenery	$ 20,000
Designer's fee	1,750
Costumes	3,000
Costume designer's fee	1,750
Stage properties	2,500
Lighting designer	1,000
Rehearsal salaries	5,000

Stage director	3,600
Stage manager	1,800
Actors' Equity Bond	15,000
Legal fees and expenses	2,500
Advertising and promotion	12,000
Press agent	900
General manager	1,500
Company manager	800
Insurance	1,500
Theatre Bond	15,000
Advance royalties to playwright	1,000
ATPAM Bond	
(for press agent and company manager)	1,200
Rehearsal hall	1,000
Office expenses	2,400
Reserve	10,000
TOTAL	$105,200

The above figures are far from maximum. A great deal more can be spent for almost every item I have mentioned, but I don't believe any producer would begin even the most simple play without $100,000 in the bank.

Then once a play has been produced and has opened and is a moderate success—let's say taking in $30,000 a week—here is the budget for the *weekly* operating expenses:

Actors	$ 7,500
Theatre (35% of gross)	10,500
Advertising	2,500
Author's royalties (10%)	3,000
Director's royalties (2%)	600
Stage manager	300
Associate stage manager	175
Press agent	400

General manager	400
Company manager	300
Office expenses	400
Taxes	750
Insurance and welfare	500
Dressers	450
Accountant	150
Rental of electrical supplies	200
Miscellaneous	250
TOTAL	$28,375

Again this is minimum, but it shows that in order to pay off the original investment, this play would have to run almost two years at $30,000 a week which is improbable because a moderate success rarely can hold to this top figure for more than eight to ten weeks (and is usually bolstered during this period by theatre parties).

A few years ago most plays and musicals that had been put together by reputable producers, directors, authors, and actors were able to survive at least the three weeks that must be played, after the official opening, before the producer and investors can receive their 40 percent interest in the film and/or television rights.

Today the economics of the theatre are so harsh that the money from a sale of such rights would not even begin to cover the losses piled up during the three-week period after a disastrous reception; even the highly publicized advance sales may not be of too much help, for they may be spread over too many months.

Budgets for musicals are now running close to three quarters of a million dollars, and operating expenses go as high as $70,000 a week. In other words, not only the instant failure but the moderate success is a total loss to the producer and his investors.

Raising the Money

Where does all the money to cover production costs come from? Men like David Merrick, Harold Prince, and Alexander Cohen have regular subscribers who can be depended upon for large amounts. Television, film, and recording companies (for the option to record "the original cast album") also invest large sums. Columbia Broadcasting System, for instance, put up all the money for the production of *My Fair Lady*. Kermit Bloomgarden prefers to involve a great number of people in the backing of his productions, and his list runs to over a hundred names, many of whom subscribe as little as $250. He says in this way he can be sure of at least a hundred boosters for his shows.

A new producer, someone starting from scratch, relies first on his personal acquaintances who have some interest in the theatre or belief in him and then sets out to hold readings of a straight play or give auditions for a musical.

A reading is often done by the author of the play, but sometimes the producer recruits three or four actors—not necessarily those who will eventually play the roles—to do the reading.

Auditions for a musical are more elaborate. Unless the composer and lyricist have the ability to present their own work— Richard Rodgers and Oscar Hammerstein auditioned *Oklahoma!;* Betty Comden and Adolph Green and Jule Styne do their own auditions—several singers are engaged, and the producer, director, or author of the book, whichever is the best storyteller, links the numbers together.

Now that musicals are so costly—the latest figure is $780,000 for Alexander Cohen's *Dear World*—the stars or principal players themselves sometimes do the numbers or at least make an appearance at the auditions.

The producer recruits his prospective backers for these auditions, usually in groups of fifty to a hundred people at a time, by circulating a prospectus to a long list of people who apparently are interested in play-investing because their names are in a book called *Angels* which is published by Leo Shull, 136 West 44th Street, New York 10036.

Keeping the Play Going

Readings and auditions also are given for the "theatre party ladies." The industrious agents who arrange parties for thousands of charities often are able to pile up enough bookings in advance to keep a production, which has received only moderately kind notices from the critics, running for weeks, even months, and in some instances have kept it on long enough to be considered a success by the public. *Variety* lists as a success only those productions which pay off their costs and make some return to the investors.

A producer frequently will keep a play open even if it is showing a small weekly loss if there seems some hope of its "building." In such a case, very often the playwright and the director are asked to reduce or entirely waive their royalties and, if Equity gives its consent, the actors take cuts in salary. The owners of the theatre, too, are asked to cooperate and take only enough to cover the bare costs of operation.

Under such conditions some plays actually have had long runs but without ever "building" sufficiently to turn a profit. And then there comes the expense of closing the show—carting away and disposing of the scenery, etc.—which can amount to another $10,000. In other words, even a long-running play or musical can be a total loss to the producer and his investors.

Nevertheless, each season there are several smash hit straight plays which pay off their original investments in fifteen to twenty weeks, and there are musical successes which, though costing more and taking longer to make a profit, continue to run for years and years and bring the producer and his backers a generous return—sometimes a fortune—not only through the box-office receipts in New York and on tour, but through the sale of motion picture, television, foreign stock, amateur rights, etc.

It is this possible bonanza that lures the producer and his backers into production and keeps the Broadway theatre alive. Gambling is attractive to many people and one of the most glamorous of gambles will always be the theatre.

Promises, Promises. Burt Bacharach, composer; Jerry Orbach and Jill O'Hara, stars; Robert Moore, director; Neil Simon author of the book adapted from the screenplay, *The Apartment.* *(Friedman-Abeles)*

15. The Director

José Ferrer once said a stage director should have "a dozen eyes and a dozen ears because there is so much for him to see and to hear." He was directing a complicated scene in *Cyrano de Bergerac* when he spoke.

The creative director has assumed increasing importance in the theatre in the last several decades. Perhaps the first time a director came in for particular attention was when David Belasco's able press agent placed various articles in the newspapers and magazines about Mr. Belasco's influence on the actors, his insistence upon realism, and the fact that in many cases, when the play was not of his authorship, he worked on the script with the playwright.

Shortly after this, critics called attention to the excellence of the Belasco direction, and then more attention in general was given to this facet of theatre art. Although critics to this day are hazy about exactly what part the director has had in the success or failure of a play, they often point out, "The director kept things moving," or "The direction was lackluster."

Unless a critic has been a director himself as, for instance, was Walter Kerr, it is very hard for him to know on opening night just where the success or failure of the direction lies.

Very often I have read reviews giving the director credit for amusing "pieces of business" and for "inventions" which the author of the play had thought out and had put in the original script.

The Director's Duties

George Abbott is famous for "keeping things moving"; Mike Nichols is truly inventive; Joshua Logan has unerring showmanship; Sir Tyrone Guthrie can do no wrong; José Quintero became famous for his successful revivals of Eugene O'Neill's plays.

But just what does a director do?

Just about everything to make or break a play. Especially today when, as I have said, so many of the new producers are promoters who more or less confine their efforts to the administration of the money and leave the all-important details of mounting the play to the director.

Directors often reshape and virtually rewrite a play before putting it into rehearsal. Sometimes if the playwright is not a particularly famous one, the director's name turns up on the finished product as coauthor. But more often even after forming the play, molding it and patting it into shape as a sculptor would a piece of clay, he receives not so much as a thank you from the author. In fact, several successful playwrights have been so unhappy with their directors that they have damned them in print. However, there are directors and playwrights who work wonderfully well together—Mike Nichols and Neil Simon, for instance—and who have a true appreciation for each other's gifts.

While the director is doing any necessary revision of the script with the author, he keeps in constant touch with the producer about the stage settings, the lighting and costume design and, of course, casting. Meetings of the producer, the director, author, general manager, and stage manager are usual, and in many cases it is the director who selects the people he finds most compatible and appropriate, since he will have so much to do with them.

The choice of scenery designer is very important to the director, because the stage settings will contribute to the plan of action which the director already has in mind. Sometimes, though not too often, the stage designer also designs the costumes. If not, then a separate designer must be selected for this important work.

Probably the leading players or stars have already been decided upon, for few producers can raise money without a star or stars to guarantee at least a modicum of interest. But sometimes the "star" is the director; Sir Tyrone Guthrie, Joshua Logan, Gower Champion, Mike Nichols, John Gielgud are all "money" names.

In a straight play, as previously pointed out, it is obligatory to send to Actors' Equity a carefully detailed list of the roles and the types of actors required for them so that the list can be posted along with the time and place for the "Equity call."

When rehearsals start, though, each director has his own approach. They all start with the reading of the play with the entire cast assembled. Jed Harris used to continue this reading of the play through the entire first week, but most directors like to get the play on its feet and start blocking the action almost at once.

From the floor plan the stage manager marks out the rehearsal hall with colored tape so that the actors can confine their actions to the areas assigned. There are chairs, tables, and benches so that the actors can start almost at once to sit or stand during particular scenes.

The director usually allows the actors to find the "comfortable moment" for sitting or rising, and if the actor is a "natural" —has a natural talent—he will unerringly find that moment. If not, it is up to the director to find it for him, especially in comedy where every movement is so important. Laughs can be killed or built by gestures and movements. The same, of course, is true of a dramatic moment, and it is the watchful director who makes sure from the very beginning that the actors are aware of these highlights and that they react properly to them.

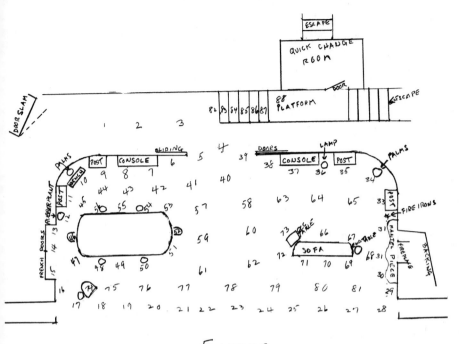

LIFE WITH FATHER

Stage manager Herman Shapiro's
system for blocking the movement of actors in the Prompt
or Master script: "It looks complicated, but I have found
it an extremely accurate and logical method.
I start my numbers at the main entrance to the set and
continue them around the set and furniture. Instead of
writing 'Father goes left stage to left end of sofa,' I
merely write the position numbers he follows, so that his
moves can be marked at specific words or directions in the
script. True, the above can be written 'F X L to L end
Sofa,' but even that is too much and not as easily under-
standable. Instead, I mark the script 'F 74-75-76-77-78-71-
70-69-sits,' if I am matching his actions to the dialogue,
or 'F 74-69-sits,' on the script's directions."

A play is a series of scenes, each one with a unity of its own: a beginning, a progression, and an end or point. The experienced or instinctive director molds these scenes carefully, blending one into the other and building them until the curtain. This gives the play its proper pace, which has nothing to do with speed.

Techniques

It is fatal for the director to allow the stars to do what I call "rattle on" without regard for the form of the scenes. George Abbott, with his reputation for fast action, is a master at defining each scene, but unknowing directors, trying to emulate him, often do not recognize the scenes within scenes and, hoping to "keep things moving," urge the actors to speak and move faster and faster; they manage to achieve only a pell-mell or frantic impression with almost a complete loss of proper values.

The forming of a scene is as important as the forming of thoughts into phrases, sentences, and paragraphs. No matter how carefully you might read an unpunctuated chapter, it would still be difficult to understand. The director must see that the play is punctuated. Otherwise he will frustrate his actors and bewilder the author who will wonder why his carefully worked-out points do not register.

As he goes along, the director and the stage manager keep the actors aware of the ultimate effect of each scene, including the light changes and any sound effects; during rehearsals, the latter are simulated by the stage manager who stamps his foot for a door slam or calls out "bell" for the telephone or doorbell.

The actors are called upon to use a great deal of imagination in the early rehearsals before there are "hand props"; it is fascinating to watch their concentration as they pick up an imaginary cup and saucer, take a sip and react to finding the tea too hot or too cold.

A film star who had had little or no stage experience walked out in panic on rehearsals of a Broadway play because, she told the director, she couldn't possibly cross the stage, put down a book, pick up and light a cigarette at the same time she was speaking a line. The skillful director finally wheedled her back and redirected the scene so that she could speak the line after putting down the book and before picking up the cigarette. The entire play was a tour de force for the director whose careful coaching went completely unnoticed by the critics who were quite impressed by the young lady's "natural talent."

Directing a Musical

Staging or directing a musical is quite a different thing from putting together a straight play. Jerome Robbins and Gower Champion act as both choreographer and director of their musicals and achieve a beautiful fluidity and integration. But usually the director works with a choreographer who not only creates the dance steps but also creates the staging of the musical numbers. And it sometimes seems, on opening night, as though these two people had never spoken to each other.

Actually very often the overall director doesn't have much chance to see the dances until they have been completed, since they are rehearsed in another rehearsal room and sometimes even in another building, and since the music director, too, is in another hall or room with his singers. So there can be quite a scramble when the director, who has been concentrating on the book, brings these facets together, especially if he is unfortunate enough to be working with a choreographer who thinks he should be staging the whole shebang.

Practical Procedures

When I direct a straight play I like to have the script read by the cast at rehearsals several times to assure myself that

Harvey Schmidt (music) and Tom Jones (words), creators of *The Fantasticks.* *(Friedman-Abeles)*

each actor is headed toward the correct characterization and knows exactly how he fits into the overall picture. Young actors, especially those steeped in The Method, are horrified when I give them "line readings," but I find that in the beginning the correct reading of a line will often illuminate the correct meaning.

I explain, when necessary, the reason and motivation—that overworked word!—for the line reading, but a talented actor needs be given only the proper inflection to understand at once.

Speaking of motivation, a Method actor once asked George Abbott what the motivation of a certain line reading that George gave him was, and George replied, "Your salary!" Another actor asked Alfred Lunt what his motivation was for crossing the stage at a certain time and Alfred answered, "To get from there to here."

At City Center where I produce more than I direct, I also do most of the casting, but always with the assistance and approval of the director. John Fearnley, who has staged most of the Rodgers and Hammerstein musicals for us, usually has very interesting and unusual ideas for casting. Gus Schirmer, director of some of our biggest hits, and I cast *Guys and Dolls* over the telephone before we even had a meeting. We confirmed our choices at the Equity call, but then Gus and I have worked together so often and for such a long long time that we know each other's taste almost by osmosis.

After greeting the cast on the first day of rehearsals, I usually sit through the first reading to assure myself that our casting has been correct, but after that I don't attend rehearsals, unless the director has a problem and particularly wants my advice or suggestions, until the first run-through. At that time I make copious notes which I give to the director.

One time as I scribbled industriously away, Gus Schirmer said to the company, "Don't worry; she's finding fault with me, not you!"

This put them at their ease, but it was not completely true, as my notes are about the actors' projection, interpretation, lack of vitality, timing, etc. I would never dream, however, of correcting the actor directly. Any producer who weakens the director's authority is the cause of ultimate chaos.

Opportunities

How does one get to be a director?

Almost all the good ones started as actors, dancers, or stage managers. In many cases, the actors became stage managers or directorial assistants and the dancers became choreographers before the responsibility of directing an entire production was given them. A few young directors have come to the professional—usually off-Broadway—theatre direct from universities where they have taken courses in stage direction. But they, too, in many cases, have had background experience as actors and/or stage managers.

Gerald Freedman who directed the original, off-Broadway production of *Hair,* the production without the nude scene which Mr. Freedman deplores—"Nudity without motivation is senseless"—is much sought after as a director of Broadway plays, but his work with the New York Shakespeare Festival is his first love. He works with very young actors, as he directs Joseph Papp's free-admission Shakespeare performances at the Delacorte Theatre in Central Park. Before meeting Mr. Papp, however, he had the usual hard theatrical row to hoe. He came to New York in his early twenties, painted scenery off Broadway, did odd jobs to make his living and says it was a very lonely life since he knew no one when he arrived and made few friends. But he stuck it out and after a season of summer stock as an actor he had the opportunity to direct a play off Broadway. His first big break came when he was engaged as dialogue director for Judy Holliday the season before her death. It was while he was working with Miss Holliday that he met Joseph Papp.

As it is for every other job in the theatre, a special talent is the all-important ingredient for directing. A good director is a good teacher, too, and has the ability to communicate his ideas with clarity, preciseness, inspiration, and even excitement.

16. Lighting and Scenic Designing

The art of lighting the stage has become highly developed in the last few decades. David Belasco was the first producer-director to make extensive use of this important factor in creation of special mood and atmosphere. He had a stage-lighting director, Louis Hartmann, who worked with him for twenty-five years, and it was Mr. Hartmann who developed many pieces of lighting equipment which are still in use today, including the "baby spot."

For an uncomplicated play with little change of time or atmosphere, the designer of the stage settings usually draws up his own lighting plot. But for a large-scale production of, say, Shakespeare, or a musical comedy, a specialist in lighting design—as it is now called—is usually brought in.

To be a professional in lighting design, it is first necessary to be a member of the United Scenic Artists of America. To become a member, you write them at 269 West 47th Street, New York 10036, or phone CI 6–8023 for application blanks. You must give a résumé of your background and credits. You are then interviewed by an examining committee and given an examination which, for full membership, tests not only creative imagination, painting, and sketching but architectural know-how. If you pass it, you enter the union on payment of an initiation fee of $1,000. This covers you as a designer of scenery, costumes, lighting, and scene painting. It may sound like a lot of money, but on one Broadway production you can earn the initiation fee plus.

An associate membership is available to those qualified only for lighting design; applicants are given an examination in lighting alone. The initiation fee is $200. Costume designers are also associate members of the United Scenic Artists of America, and take an examination covering only their field. The initiation fee for them is $300.

In order to pass these tests, you need not only a great natural talent, but a background of actual experience which usually is gained in work on university productions and with amateur groups and in some of the summer theatres where nonunion designers are welcome.

Where Crafts Are Taught

If you are an artist and it is your ambition to design for the stage, it is imperative that you attend a university which has a special course in this most demanding theatre art. One of the best of these is Yale University. Other colleges that give courses in scenic design are Carnegie Institute of Technology in Pittsburgh; Northwestern University, Chicago; Baylor University, Waco, Texas; University of California, Berkeley and Los Angeles; Stanford University, Palo Alto, California; and all universities that have their own theatres on or near the campus where shows are produced by university students of the drama and/or their guests.

When the course is completed, if you have been fortunate enough to have had one of your designs used in a successful university production, you may be accepted as an apprentice by a theatre designer who is working on several productions at the same time and needs fresh talent. Or even better, in my opinion, you may find work with a summer theatre where you will immediately be able to use your knowledge and skill; this practical experience will make the United Scenic Artists union examination much less terrifying.

When you are gaining this important background, work

with the director at the theatre as much as possible. I take it for granted that at the university you learned how to read a script and from it to conceive an all-important "idea" of the entire production.

Most designers are gifted with the ability to visualize instantly a setting, with all of the proper exits, sight-lines, sources of light, etc. But in most summer theatres, the program will consist mainly of "revivals," and the director will want you to re-create the set more or less exactly like the original.

Don't scorn this work because it doesn't call upon your creative imagination. You will find that some very knotty problems have been solved with ingenuity and flair. You can go over your own thoughts on the same subject and try to come up with better solutions. If you do—or even think you do—be sure to discuss them with the director. If he goes on to stage a Broadway or even off-Broadway production, he might well insist that you go with him; then, the first all-important step will have been taken.

Difficulties in Getting Started on Broadway

Designing for off Broadway calls for great ingenuity as space is limited and so is money. You will, of course, do your own lighting and this too calls for ingenuity as equipment is reduced to a minimum because of cost.

The newspaper critics know this and often comment in their columns on the work of the designer; their praise can be enormously helpful in gaining you entrance to the more lucrative field of Broadway design.

Even after a designer has met all the qualifications of the union, it is still not easy for him to get that first all-important opportunity to design a Broadway show. Producers and directors like to rely on people with whom they have worked previously or whose designs have already received acclaim.

This is especially important because the union requires that a contract be signed with the designer *before* he submits sketches or even ideas for the scenery to be used.

Final sketches and models of the scenery are then sent to the United Scenic Artists where they are duly registered and stamped. Each and every costume design also is thus protected.

The producer, too, is protected by the union. After he puts up the bond or money for the designer's total fees (this money is held by the union and paid out by it at specified times, usually one third upon signing of the contract, one third midway in the work, and the balance when the play is opened), he signs the contract which specifies the duties of the designers.

These duties include the making of blueprints, sketches, and models. Also the supervision of the building and painting of the settings, the selection of stage properties—furniture, draperies, and ornaments—and the designer's attendance at dress rehearsals, tryouts, and previews.

Importance of Good Set Design

Everyone who has worked in the theatre for any length of time knows that a stage setting can help or hinder a production. Often cast members have remarked, "We felt we had a hit at the final run-through on the bare stage, but once we were saddled with those damn sets, we felt overpowered and all the magic seemed to evaporate."

I have never seen a play or musical ruined by underproduction, but I have seen many fatally overproduced. Lavish scenery and costumes, too colorful, too detailed, too gimmicky can smother a frail and lovely theme.

All too many Broadway productions today are overproduced. This is especially true of the musicals with their elaborate moving scenery—the sets that change before your eyes—and their fancy costumes that all too often interfere with the

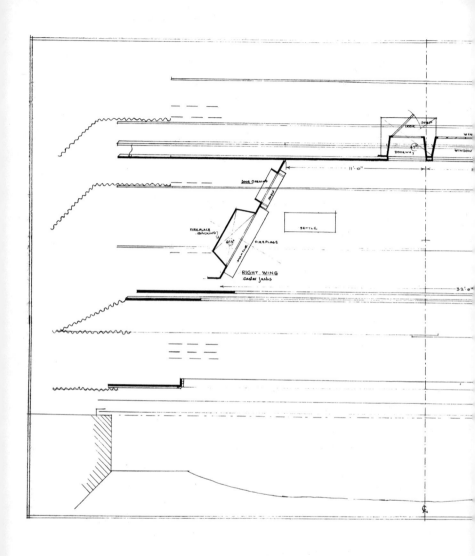

Ground plan for *Brigadoon*.
The plan was designed by Oliver Smith and drawn by Peggy Clark.

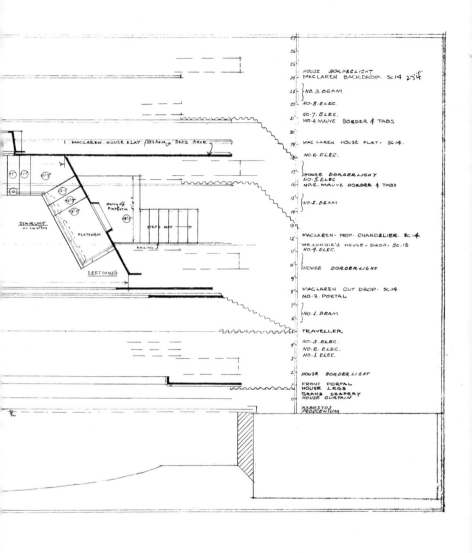

27'
26'
25'
24'   HOUSE BORDERLIGHT
     MACLAREN BACK DROP. Sc. 14 2'-3"
23' } NO. 3. BEAM
22' } NO. 8. ELEC.
21'   NO. 7. ELEC.
     NO. 4 MAUVE BORDER & TABS
20'
19'   MACLAREN HOUSE FLAT. Sc. 14.
18'   NO. 6. ELEC.
17' } HOUSE BORDERLIGHT
     NO. 5. ELEC.
16'   NO. 2. MAUVE BORDER & TABS
15' } NO. 2. BEAM
14'
13'   MACLAREN - PROP. CHANDELIER. Sc. 14.
12'   MR. LUNDIE'S HOUSE - DROP. Sc. 13
11'   NO. 4. ELEC.
10' } HOUSE BORDERLIGHT
9'
8'   MACLAREN CUT DROP. Sc. 14
     NO. 2. PORTAL
7' } NO. 1. BEAM
6'
     TRAVELLER
5'
4'   NO. 3. ELEC.
     NO. 2. ELEC.
3'   NO. 1. ELEC.
2'   HOUSE BORDER LIGHT
1'   FRONT PORTAL
     HOUSE LEGS
     GRAND DRAPERY
0'   HOUSE CURTAIN
     ASBESTOS
     PROSCENIUM

1 MACLAREN HOUSE FLAT (flashing) SETS HERE

Carry off
Platform

STAIR UNIT
on casters

PLATFORM

STEP OFF

RAILING

LEFT WING

PL

choreographer's basic conception of line and form. There have been several famous musicals which had to get completely new sets of costumes for the dancers during the out-of-town try-outs because the dances could not be performed in the swaddling clothes that had been designed for them.

Lighting

Abe Feder has been famous as a master of lighting ever since his work with Orson Welles on the 1937 production of *Dr. Faustus*. Since then he has done the lighting on some three hundred important productions, including *My Fair Lady*.

Today his commercial work absorbs most of his time and talents, but the theatre is still his first love, because it was at the theatre that he first became fascinated with lights. He and his sister had gone to see the famous magician known as the Great Thurston at a theatre in Milwaukee. He says: "Colored dazzling lights all over the stage! I went home in a dream. I couldn't sleep for two nights; I saw the lights whenever I closed my eyes. I have been obsessed with light ever since."

As soon as he was able to, he went to the Carnegie Institute of Technology in Pittsburgh, preceded by a letter of recommendation from his high school principal who described him as "a kid with a passion for lighting."

Much of his time at Carnegie Tech was spent in lighting the shows of the Drama Department, but since his teachers refused to recognize light as a separate architectural element he left college at the end of his sophomore year to devote himself solely to lighting.

His first professional job was with the Goodman Theater, a repertory group in Chicago. He considered—and still considers—the stage the perfect place for trying out his ideas. "Everybody can see the difference between a well-lit and a badly lit play," he says. "In a play, the slightest mistake shows up, and the whole character of the show may be changed by the lights. Stage lighting is a mixture of science and art. Scene follows scene. You must rely on speed, flexibility, and a minimum of machinery. I learned to discipline myself in the theater. Simplicity of impression is important. . . . Light is a tricky thing. It can be a blessing if you know how to tame it and a monster if you let it get out of hand."

When Feder came to New York at twenty-one, he was the youngest lighting expert in the business and already well-known for his "fanaticism." He worked with the Federal Theater during the depression and that was a busy and happy period for him—a dramatic show one night, an opera or a ballet the next. He had over a million dollars' worth of equipment at his disposal, and it was during this time that he enjoyed his first great success, the Orson Welles' *Dr. Faustus.*

Mr. Feder was good enough to give us the following layout for a lighting designer to follow for a realistic play:

Steps in Lighting:

A. Read the Script.
   1. Talk to director and designer. Understand style, purpose and kind of production. Find out length of time of rehearsal, and budget available for lighting equipment.

B. Visit the Theatre.
   1. Study the house: its limitations. Possible board control and changes to be made if necessary. Where can you hang your equipment? Is there any compromise to be made because of the nature of the house and the style of the show?

C. Break Down Script on Paper.
   1. You know your script fairly well: the style of the show, the effects desired. Now scene by scene, begin to take

notes on the time of day, the sources of motivating light, the mood of the scene, the distribution of the light in the acting areas, and on the actors. Sketch in the equipment you will need for these purposes.

2. Having done this for the whole play, try to visualize a ground plan of equipment which will be adequate for the whole show, from the point of view of economy of operation, flexibility of use from scene to scene, and subtlety of esthetic effect: think of *color*, and *quality* of lighting.

D. Draw Your Ground Plan, and Layout of Equipment.
1. Take your lighting plan to the director. Explain it. Change it if necessary. Get it approved.

E. Attend Rehearsals.
1. "Soak up" the show. Watch it for mood and visualize the effects you will want to create. Begin in your mind to hang your equipment, and plan its operation. Coordination of operation is all important: simplicity above all.
2. By the time you are ready to order equipment (or use what is available) the layout is fairly clear; the method of running the board is also becoming clearer; if there is anything tricky in the show, you now know where it will be, and have an idea of how you can get the particular effect.

F. Order and Installation of Equipment.
1. Make sure of your source of power and adequate control; the amount of actual electrical load capacity available; the number of portable switchboards necessary.
2. Lamps are hung by the stage electrician according to the lighting plan.
3. Lamps are focused by him film by film. Color frames are installed. Basically, the show is now ready for writing your first cue sheet.
4. Hold basic light rehearsals for scene movement.

G. First Rehearsals of Light and Actors and Scenery.
1. Without disturbing rehearsals, start feeding in the lights on the scenes. Take your notes for your first cue sheet. (This will be changed fifty times, but don't worry about it.) The director will start arguing about effects. Keep him happy, and make the necessary changes.
2. Lamps will need refocusing and colors will have to be changed. Possibly different setup of the ground plan may be necessary; now is the time to find out and do it.
3. At the end of this period (two days to a week), a fairly smooth cue sheet exists, and the show can be run. Refinements and changes creep in, and are added as you go along. Questions of color, mood, effects, and dimmer readings and operations have been almost solved.

H. Dress Rehearsals, Previews.
1. Emphasis is on smoothness of operation. The light must be a co-ordinate part of the show, unobtrusive and subtle, a single efficient part of the whole production. The light will enhance the beauty and meaning of the scenery, increase the esthetic effect of the whole production, and provide enough illumination to see all the actors plainly.
2. By the last preview the board operation is almost smoothly perfect. The most important decisions on effects have been made, so that everybody is happy: director, designer, and yourself.

The show is ready for opening night.

17. Publicity and Public Relations

The terms public relations and publicity are often confused even by the publicists themselves, many of whom mistakenly call themselves "directors of public relations" simply because to them it sounds like a more dignified and highfalutin' title than press agent, as theatre publicity people are called.

If anyone personifies public relations in the theatre, it is the box-office man or treasurer who deals directly with the public. It is too bad that they are often so overworked and irritated toward the end of a long day that their pleasant manner wears off and their reputation for general churlishness is all too well borne out.

I should say, too, that the doorman, the ushers, and the house manager (the man who actually runs the theatre) all are doing public relations. Unfortunately many of these people who have direct contact with the public, the people who buy the theatre tickets and support the industry, do not realize their important link. In fact, public relations is something all too often ignored in the commercial theatre.

In the new and rapidly expanding "cultural centers," in which generally nonprofit and tax-deductible institutions depend upon grants and donations to augment their income, public relations is recognized as vitally important and the public image of these institutions is carefully maintained.

The public image is also maintained through the kind of

publicity an organization receives. While notoriety and even scandal never seem to hurt and often help in the commercial theatre, it is carefully guarded against and sometimes even skillfully hidden by the semipublic institutions.

Their publicity directors, therefore, must have a sense of public relations—relationship with the public—as well as background and experience in the field of theatre publicity.

The Press Agent

A Broadway or commercial theatrical publicity director is called a press agent and like the company manager must be a member of ATPAM—the Association of Theatrical Press Agents and Managers. It is not easy to qualify for membership in this craft union. To become a member, you must first serve an apprenticeship with a member for sixty weeks which can be consecutive or spread over a three-year period. While you are an apprentice, you can work with the agent as a writer, secretary, typist, or general office helper. After the sixty-week learning period, and upon the payment of $500, you are admitted to the union.

ATPAM allows an agent to cover only one play at a time by himself, and so he must engage an associate if his producer brings out a second play or if he wants to work for more than one producer, which is allowed, as press agents are more or less autonomous. An associate also must be an ATPAM member.

The minimum fee for a Broadway press agent is $286.50 a week, but very few of the experienced and better-known members of ATPAM work for minimum. After all he must pay his associate *his* minimum which is $185. (Off-Broadway is $175 for the original press agent and $144.50 for an associate.)

The press agent is limited by the rules of ATPAM to handle a maximum of six shows, on or off Broadway, with three associates. He can handle three shows with one associate; five shows with two associates, but that extra sixth show needs a third associate.

Associates are not limited to working on only one particular show. They assist the senior press agent on all of them, but can work with only one agent at a time.

Publicity Outlets

There are only three metropolitan newspapers in New York today and they give very little space to theatre news. There was a time when a Broadway press agent had to be a good writer, and feature stories about a play's personalities—stars, producer, author, director—were eagerly accepted for publication if well written. Today space is so limited that only actual news or salient features about a production get squeezed in.

But there is much more than the newspapers for the press agent to service: television, radio, the press services, news and other magazines, the hotel publications, the trade publications, and *Playbill,* the official program for New York theatres. (There are eighty-three such outlets on our City Center first-night press list.) There are the interviews to be arranged, the "house boards" to be made up, the mailing piece, or brochure, to be written, the advertising to be laid out, and a "photo call" to be set.

The official "photo call" is made, as I have said, shortly after the actors have their costumes and the scenery has been put in place, but since the press agent must have photographs to send out even before this time because magazine and some other deadlines frequently are six weeks or more before publication, "rehearsal shots" are often made with the actors dressed in approximate costumes and photographed against makeshift scenery. These are more or less posed shots. But the best photos made today are "candids" taken by an experienced theatrical photographer during an actual performance—usually the dress rehearsal.

These photographs are then "backed": a typewritten page giving the name of the play and pertinent facts such as the name of the theatre, date of opening, etc., and of course a list of the actors included in the scene is attached to the back of the photograph. Photos are then sent out wherever they may be used—newspapers, magazines, television stations.

Another set of photographs is used to decorate the theatre lobby, and enlargements are frequently mounted outside the theatre if there is space for them.

"House boards" are the announcements outside the theatre which give the name of the play, the producer, the stars, director, and others connected with the production. These are usually hand-lettered by experts and are often very beautiful. Equity demands that everyone engaged as an actor must be listed on one of these boards and if it is a big cast, this usually is a replica of the listing in *Playbill.*

Making up the program for *Playbill* is a press agent's headache, for the billing must be exact, not only in position and in size of type used for the names of everyone connected with a production, but also in the writing and the order of the biographies in the "Who's Who" section.

Fortunately Equity now has another good rule, which is that each actor must okay, in writing, his biography as it is prepared by the press agent, and also he must okay the proofs before the program is printed.

Fortunately, too, for the press agent, when it comes to the advertisements in the newspapers and magazines, he has the help of people who specialize in theatrical advertising and who can carry out his ideas for illustration, typography, and general layout of the material submitted to them. Here again, the all-important billing problem can turn into a small nightmare for the press agent unless the order of precedence, the size of type and so on are correct down to the last agate line, especially in the case of stars, important playwrights, and directors.

These billing details are spelled out on the typewritten "rider" attached to the Equity contract. Any infraction can be reported to Equity, and the contract can be considered broken and the star can leave, or a fine can be imposed on the producer, which usually amounts to two weeks' salary.

After the play opens, and if it receives good notices, there is the "quote ad" to be made up—sometimes a full page—of the excerpts from all the praising comments. These large quote ads generally are used in the newspapers only in the case of a smash hit where the notices really are "raves." Very often, in the case of mild approbation by the critics, it is impossible to extract enough favorable lines to do the play any good. That is the difference between a nice notice and a "money notice."

If the play is going to have an out-of-town tryout tour, then a great deal of all this work is done in duplicate or triplicate or more, depending on the number of cities to be visited.

Who Become Press Agents?

The old-time press agents were virtually all newspapermen originally, but the apprentice system has done away with that and most of the new members are bright college graduates who start as office assistants or secretaries to producers or press agents. Since Equity summer theatres and Equity resident companies throughout the country must use ATPAM members, these young, well-trained publicity directors—as they now usually like to be called—are in constant demand.

Touring and national companies of a Broadway hit do better with a seasoned old "advance man" type of press agent, and there are many of these who have spent a lifetime in the hinterlands and prefer it that way. Their writing ability does come in handy as feature stories are sought by the out-of-town newspapers; in the case of one-night stands, the press agent sometimes is asked to submit a "review" of his production to the paper *in toto.*

The Advance Man

The advance press agent on a national tour, like the press agent for a Broadway play on a tryout tour, makes *all* the necessary arrangements.

He checks in with the manager of the theatre where the attraction is to play, provides him with a time schedule of the arrival of the scenery, and makes arrangements for its local delivery. In the old days the company and scenery traveled by train and in the case of a very large musical they still do. But for short trips and straight plays, it is customary to ship the scenery by truck while the actors travel by plane.

He meets with the theatre's local press agent, if there is one, and makes sure that the program copy which he has sent ahead by mail has been received and is being correctly used.

He makes sure the advance billing in the front of the theatre is correct and that all photographs are being displayed.

He makes hotel reservations for the actors.

He visits the drama editor and/or critic of the local newspaper, makes sure that whatever material he has sent by mail has been or will be used, and leaves additional photographs and stories for future use.

He visits the local television and radio stations and sets up interviews for the star or stars.

He uses his ingenuity, experience, and contacts with women's clubs, schools, universities, etc., to arouse interest in his production.

Usually he stays through the opening night performance and part of the following day in order to make up any necessary "quote ads" and then he moves on to the next town on the tour.

If anything goes wrong—if the hotel rooms are not satisfactory, the publicity or billing not to the star's liking, or any detail left undone—the poor press agent is vilified. There is a famous theatre story about a great star who was touring for the first time. Everywhere she went she found things to complain about and when she asked who was responsible, she always was told, "The advance man." One night, just as she was about to make her first entrance, she slipped and fell, and as she went down she was heard to mutter, "Damn that advance man!"

What Makes a Good Press Agent?

The most successful theatrical publicists or press agents are not those who try for the spectacular newsbreak, but the ones who can be depended upon for trustworthy information and prompt cooperation.

Of course personality, diplomacy, camaraderie, and humor are all to the good in the press agent, but it is no longer necessary to hobnob at a bar. The hard-drinking newspaperman of *The Front Page* and *Gentlemen of the Press* is a thing of the past. Everyone is too busy, competition is too tough, and the pace is too swift.

In New York, as I mentioned before, with only three newspapers and space at a premium, column items are often used by press agents to keep the name of a play or the players before the public. Columnists are happy to have amusing, short anecdotes—Leonard Lyons in *The New York Post* especially—bits of gossip, or unusual information. A good deal of this material for the columns is manufactured, but the columnists don't seem to hold it against the press agents who depend more on imagination than on fact. There actually are some minor publicists who make a business of placing column items; sometimes they are employed by the big-time theatre publicists who have no patience with this phase of publicity.

The press agent has an interesting life—one of the most interesting in the theatre—and his experience is a wonderful steppingstone for his becoming a producer. But it is a difficult life, almost a twenty-four-hour job, and like the poor "advance man," he is apt to get all the blame and very little gratitude.

Part Four: The Play's the Thing

18. Writing for the Theatre

Playwrights seem to be born with a special sense of theatre. Many of the best of them can write only in play form and are virtually incapable of putting together a narrative piece.

George Bernard Shaw said that playwriting was the most difficult form of communication devised by man. He told me that he much preferred narrative writing and that putting his thoughts into play form was exhausting. But he wrote many plays, he said, because he felt sure that the ideas he wanted to express would have more impact when spoken than when read.

"When I stand at the back of the theatre and hear my words being listened to by a packed house, I am rewarded for all the hours, days and months I spent painstakingly arranging them, for play-writing is not so much writing as building and that is why playwright is spelled W R I G H T not write. Plays are wrought, not written."

Only a few successful novelists have been able to turn out fine theatre works. I once had a four-hour luncheon with Ernest Hemingway during which I evidently convinced him that his ear for dialogue should lead him to playwriting. Shortly after that pleasant meeting, he wrote *The Fifth Column*, a play about the Spanish Civil War which was produced by the Theatre Guild, after having been adapted by Benjamin Glazer.

It was not a success. Franchot Tone, who starred in it, and

Playwright Joseph Heller with costars Jason Robards and Diana Sands at a rehearsal of *We Bombed in New Haven*. *(Bert Andrews)*

several other theatre people who had read the original, said that Hemingway's script with all its faults—"too long; too talky"—might have had a better chance. Later Hemingway told me he hadn't enjoyed playwriting and would never attempt it again. He never did.

Rachel Crothers, who was the first successful woman playwright with twenty-six hits in twenty-six years, once told me, "I never start to write until I am well-acquainted with all of my characters and the story they are going to tell. Then I describe the stage setting as briefly as possible and let the play begin. I write down the words I hear my characters say and as 'stage business' I simply put down what they do."

It sounded easy, and to her it was because she had always, from the time she first started to write, thought in play form. She was never taught, she told me, and she had seen only a few church plays and one or two stock productions when, in her teens, she wrote her first play, which was a success.

I was John Golden's press agent, production assistant, casting director, and general factotum when he produced two of Miss Crothers' biggest hits—As Husbands Go and When Ladies Meet—and I often spent weekends with her at her home in Connecticut while she was working.

She would sit in bed with a thick pad of yellow paper on her lap and a glassful of sharp pencils by her side and write rapidly in a large, easily decipherable scrawl—so rapidly that the yellow pages seemed to fly out of her lap and onto the floor. When she had finished, her secretary would pick them up—they were carefully numbered—and type them out for her.

Miss Crothers rarely made a change after that until she went into production. She directed all of her own plays and edited them after she heard them read.

"The sound of the play is all-important," she once told me. "It is like the orchestration of a composition and to me directing is very similar to conducting. I often turn my back on a scene and just listen to it. If it sounds right, I know it is right."

I also worked closely at this time with another popular playwright of the 20s and 30s, Frank Craven. He used to come into my office in the John Golden Theatre and say, "Jeannie, do you have a moment or two to rattle off a theme I have in mind?" (I was a very fast typist; still am.) Frank loved to dictate directly to the typewriter. He would stride up and down, smoking his pipe, and between puffs act out a scene which would later appear on the stage virtually unchanged.

He wrote the entire play *That's Gratitude!*, which was a great success, in just this way and in a remarkably short time. He said he not only liked to dictate to me because I was a good typist, but because I was also a good audience. I often laughed so hard and so long that I "stopped the show" as he put it.

It wasn't just because of the situation or lines, but because of his tremendous gift as a great and amusing actor. When *That's Gratitude!*, in which he starred, became a hit, he surprised and delighted me by allotting me part of his royalties.

Tennessee Williams and Harold Pinter both acted before they turned to playwriting, although neither achieved particular eminence as an actor. Tennessee Williams' first writing success was *The Glass Menagerie*. I saw it when it was done originally by Margo Jones in Dallas. Margo was the first producer to recognize Tennessee's—or Tom's, as he likes to be called—genius.

After the play's mild success in Dallas, Margo took it to Chicago where only one critic, the dauntless Claudia Cassidy, recognized its worth, but the two women kept it running until Eddie Dowling decided to bring it to Broadway starring Laurette Taylor—and the rest is theatre history.

Williams' second play, *You Touched Me*, was a delightful fantasy, but it was produced, directed, and acted in such a realistic style that it achieved only a fair success. I said this to Audrey Wood, Williams' playbroker, and I added that I thought only women should produce his plays.

A woman did produce his next play but to my chagrin it wasn't I. It was Irene Selznick, and the play was *A Streetcar Named Desire.*

Another woman, Cheryl Crawford, produced *Cat on a Hot Tin Roof,* also a great success, and his *Sweet Bird of Youth* and *Period of Adjustment.*

Mr. Williams says he believes all plays come out of some inner tension in the playwright himself. He is concerned about a problem and that concern works itself out in the form of creative writing. He writes his plays rapidly on a typewriter, but often rewrites them four or five times before he is satisfied. And he often rewrites his plays even after they have been produced. *The Milk Train Doesn't Stop Here Any More* was produced twice, in two versions: the first with Hermione Baddeley and the second with Tallulah Bankhead. Neither was a success, yet Richard Burton and Elizabeth Taylor made the play into the film *Boom!* (Not a success either.)

Harold Pinter still appears from time to time as an actor and now also is a director, having started this latter career on Broadway with *The Man in the Glass Booth.*

Pinter says he wrote his first play in one act, *The Room,* in four days and it was produced with such success at the University of Bristol, England, that he immediately started work on a full-length play, *The Birthday Party.*

The London critics didn't understand it any better than I did the first time it was produced on the West End, and massacred it. But oddly enough, when Pinter himself directed the second West End production a few months later, it was a hit. Its Broadway production also did well.

I, like many others, look for symbolism and hidden meaning in his characters but Pinter says, "There is nothing there you do not see."

In a program note on *The Room* and another of his excellent one-act plays, *The Dumbwaiter,* when they were produced in London, Pinter wrote: "There are no hard distinctions between what is real and what is unreal, nor between what is true and what is false."

The Caretaker first made him known to the American public and gave Donald Pleasence the opportunity to play an unforgettable character and immediately made him an important star in the Broadway constellation.

The Homecoming has been Pinter's longest-running American success, and it also had two superbly written characters, brilliantly played by his wife, Vivien Merchant, and Paul Rogers.

Arthur Miller started playwriting while at the University of Michigan and during that time one of his plays was a prize-winner in a Theatre Guild competition, but it was never produced. His first professional work was writing plays for radio, and he has said that this was a very important experience for him.

When *All My Sons* was produced on Broadway and won the Drama Critics' Award, he was well on his way, but *Death of a Salesman* put him at the very top of American playwrights. It was not only a popular smash hit, but it won him both the Pulitzer Prize and the Drama Critics' Award.

Miller says he writes and rewrites a play a thousand times in his head before he puts a word on paper. Then he says it all goes very quickly, sometimes taking only five or six weeks to complete.

Although William Inge never wrote a play until he was thirty, he taught drama for five years at Stephens College for Women in Columbia, Missouri. Later he became the drama and music critic for *The St. Louis Star-Times,* and since Tennessee Williams' parents lived in St. Louis, Inge took a particular interest in Williams when *The Glass Menagerie* opened in Chicago.

Tennessee came to St. Louis to visit his parents, and Inge interviewed him. At this meeting Inge discussed his own playwriting ambitions. Tennessee encouraged him and promised to help him. When Inge had finished the first draft of *Come Back, Little Sheba,* Tennessee sent it to his playbroker, Audrey Wood, who sold it almost immediately to the Theatre Guild. It was tried out at the Westport Country Playhouse, which Lawrence Langner—head of the Guild—owned.

It was not a success; that is, it didn't do good business. Perhaps it was because its stars, Shirley Booth and Sydney Blackmer, were not "draws" at that time and its author was unknown. During the middle of its week's run, my friend Robert Garland, who was the critic of the *Journal-American,* asked if I would go up to Westport with him to see a play by a new playwright who Audrey Wood felt had great talent.

After seeing this magnificent play, I couldn't believe my good fortune when Shirley Booth told me that the Guild was dropping it. I told her and Sydney that I would definitely bring it to Broadway. I called Audrey Wood the next morning but she said Theresa Helburn—Lawrence Langner's partner in the Theatre Guild—had already called her. Miss Helburn said she had heard that I wanted the play and that "if Jean thinks that much of it, the Guild might as well take a chance on it. It won't cost much. We already have the set and it won't need a tryout tour."

It was, in fact, the least costly of any Theatre Guild production and, although it ran only six months, it turned them a pretty profit. It made Shirley Booth a top-ranking star and put William Inge firmly on the map as a gifted American playwright. It is still my favorite Inge play, although his second play, *Picnic,* won the Pulitzer Prize, the Drama Critics' Award, and the Donaldson Award.

Inge says that sometimes it is a character, a memory, an experience, or just a mood that impels him to put that blank sheet of paper in the typewriter and start with those magic words, ACT I. He says he doesn't outline a play. He has to work it out on the typewriter. Then he rewrites—not the whole thing, he says, just bits and pieces.

The playwright consciously or unconsciously has the players for the leading parts in mind when he writes a play, and the important playwright usually gets them. He sits in on the auditions and also on conferences with the scene designer, costume designer, etc.

The "Last Word" on Playwrighting

So . . . how do you write a play?

Not a single successful playwright has been able to give more than a hint. But they all say that you must sit down and write, and if necessary, write again and keep on writing.

What to write about seems no problem these days. The more cockamanie the idea you have, the better it may be.

It has been said that the day of the "well-made play" is past, but I don't believe this. You still must have interesting characters with whom the audience can make some sort of personal identification. They must still be involved in a story which has a beginning, a middle, and an end. They must still characterize themselves by their lines.

If you have the wonderful urge to write a play, don't put it off. Grab that pencil and some yellow paper or stick a sheet in your typewriter and begin—ACT I.

And while you work, remember that any person who has written or is engaged in writing a dramatic play or musical work may apply for membership in the Dramatists Guild by writing to the Guild, 234 West 44th Street, New York 10036. Their contract is a wonderful protection for the writer.

19. Getting Your Play Produced

For many years the cry was, "Where are the playwrights?" Today they are everywhere, and opportunities for them are greater than ever before—although not on Broadway. Off Broadway and off-off Broadway present dozens of full-length plays and many one-act plays each year, and new playwrights are being encouraged, guided, and produced by dedicated groups, directors, and producers. Much of all this activity leads nowhere. The basic talent is just not there in too many cases, but at least playwrights do have a market and a showcase which did not exist until a comparatively short time ago.

On the other hand, thirty years ago—even twenty-five years ago—many of the plays now being presented in church basements, coffeehouses, lofts, remodeled stores, and narrow brownstones would have found a showcase on Broadway. Today it is economics that keeps them off, not disinterest or obtuseness on the part of the Broadway showmen.

Then, too, the taste and standards of critics and playgoers are at an all-time high. Television is greatly responsible for this. Entertainment can be found on the home screen without cost, without the aggravation of transportation or inclement weather, and so it is only the "must see" attraction on Broadway that lures sufficient playgoers to the box office to make the headache, the heartaches, and the astronomical cost of a new play worthwhile.

The mortality rate is high and ever higher on and even off

Playwright Brian Friel, actor Art Carney, and director Hilton Edwards, shown prior to the opening of the comedy, *Lovers. (Bert Andrews)*

Broadway. The "nice" play, the "pleasant" musical, and the "interesting" drama close immediately. Faint praise is a death blow. It must be "the wildest, most hilarious comedy," "a masterpiece of a musical," "an unforgettable, soul-searing drama" to sell tickets. The "money notices."

Without these notices, it is economically impossible to try to find an audience. People just will not come. You can't even give tickets away. But that gem of a script which will get the notices is always somewhere being written or waiting to be read, and it could be yours.

Finding an Agent

Most of the Broadway producers return unsolicited manuscripts unread and will accept only work submitted, and highly recommended, by a recognized literary agent or playbroker. And it is almost as hard to interest an agent in your play as it is to find a willing producer.

Most agencies charge a reading fee. The small amount asked, usually $25.00, is well worth the investment because if the agent or broker finds talent in your writing or your basic idea he will take a personal interest in you and your work and give you the benefit of his great experience and far-reaching connections.

If you have been fortunate enough to achieve an off-Broadway or even an off-off-Broadway production on your own, an agent may seek you out. Some of them go searching the small theatres for writing talent but the majority wait for the talent to come to them.

The New Dramatists' Committee

In 1950, The New Dramatists' Committee was formed. A young playwright, Michaela O'Harra, had the idea of starting an educational program for playwrights, and the first person who took an interest in her plan was the late Robert Garland, at that time the powerful drama critic of the *New York Journal-American.* He saw to it that doors were opened for her.

One of the first established playwrights to realize the benefits such a program could have for writers was Howard Lindsay. He and his partner, Russell Crouse, and Miss O'Harra enlisted Richard Rodgers, Moss Hart, John Golden, John Wharton, and Oscar Hammerstein II, and The New Dramatists' Committee was started in the donated offices they still occupy in the New York City Center. The "donation" by the way was proposed to the City Center Board by Mrs. Henry Morgenthau, Jr.

The aim of this Committee was and is to help dedicated playwrights write better plays. Playwrights who are accepted as members attend craft discussions in which leading directors, scenic designers, lighting designers, and stage managers discuss their work. But the most valuable service the Committee offers a young playwright is the experience of seeing his play "on its feet," presented by professional directors, actors, and theatre technicians before an invited audience.

There are also round-table discussions among the young playwrights themselves, often with leading playwrights, producers, and directors joining in. Then, too, members are sometimes invited to observe a Broadway production from the first rehearsal through out-of-town tryouts to opening night. A New Dramatist, as a guest of Broadway and off-Broadway managers, can see virtually all current productions each season.

Several hundred playwrights have become members of the Committee, among them two Pulitzer Prizewinners—Joseph Kramm, whose *The Shrike* won the award in 1952, and William Inge, whose *Picnic* received the Pulitzer Prize in 1953. Member Robert Anderson turned out *Tea and Sympathy*, 1953–54, Joseph Hayes, *The Desperate Hours*, 1954–55, Paddy Chayefsky, *Middle of the Night*, 1955–56, Ronald Alexander, *Holiday for Lovers*, 1956–57, William Gibson, *Two for the*

Seesaw, 1957–58. Not a season has gone by without several plays being done on Broadway, and even more of them off Broadway, by Committee members.

To become a New Dramatist, you must submit one full-length play and other written works—one-act plays, stories, sketches, television programs, etc.—or two full-length plays. Your play or plays then will be read and passed upon by several groups.

If the first-level group approves of your work, it is then read by the second-level group, and finally it goes to the Board of Governors, at least two of whom must endorse it.

About 250 plays are read each year, yet in 1966–67, only nine new members were admitted. However, more than 450 playwrights have been accepted as members over the years.

If you are fortunate enough—and talented enough—to be accepted as a member of The New Dramatists' Committee, you will be well on your way to a production of your play, for literary agents keep an eye on new members and attend many of the staged readings.

The Playwrights' Unit

Another important workshop organization that is a remarkable outlet for new playwrights is The Playwrights' Unit, organized by Richard Barr, Edward Albee and Clinton Wilder in 1962, after their great successes off and on Broadway with Mr. Albee's plays. Eighty-three new plays (many in one act) have been showcased by the Unit and have served to introduce and encourage Megan Terry, Sanford Wilson, Sam Shepard, Jean-Claude van Itallie, LeRoi Jones and Mart Crowley, among others.

Mr. Crowley's play, *The Boys in the Band,* is far and away the biggest hit brought out by The Playwrights' Unit. Produced by Mr. Barr and William Woodward, Jr., it is still selling out at the start of its second year off Broadway, and the London West End production is soon to open. Film rights were sold for $500,000, with the understanding that Mr. Crowley would write the screenplay and produce the film and that Robert Moore, the original director, who has since staged David Merrick's big hit, *Promises, Promises,* would direct.

Plays may be submitted to the Unit at 15 Vandam Street, New York, N. Y. 10003. They are read by Charles Gnys, who directs most of the showcase productions, and if he likes them they are then read by Mr. Barr and Mr. Albee for final approval. The productions are completely professional, with scenery, lighting, costumes and talented actors.

Options

Many plays are optioned by producers but never produced. Some producers do playwrights a great disservice by tying up their plays for several years and then finally letting them drop, because of the inability to sign a name director or star. But most frequently it is because of failure to raise the necessary financing.

If your play is under option to a reputable producer, and time begins to go by, it is a good idea to get in touch with him either in person or by telephone or by mail. Suggestions for casting or even for money raising are not out of order on your part.

Financial Gains

If your play is produced, it can be a source of considerable financial return to you, even if it proves a total loss to the producer.

Part of the reason is that there are over 100,000 amateur theatre companies in the United States. John Patrick told me that his unsuccessful comedy, *The Curious Savages,* brought him over a quarter of a million dollars from this market alone.

Edward Albee's *A Delicate Balance,* which was not particularly well received on Broadway, has been playing all over the world, and the same is true of his *Everything in the Garden.* But then there is always a market for Albee, even for minor Albee.

Serious plays by lesser-known dramatists do not fare so well, but comedies, even those disparaged by the critics, often find their way to the summer and winter stock circuits and into the amateur theatres in many lands.

Sixty percent of all money paid for a play by a film or television company goes to the author; if the production has run more than three weeks, 40 percent of the film and television income goes to the producer who in turn pays 20 percent to his investors. If the play closes before three weeks, all money from any subsidiary source whatever goes to the playwright.

With cultural centers blossoming in virtually every major city in the United States, the opportunities for a writing career in the theatre are greater than ever. The resident repertory company is beginning to flourish, and the demand for writing talent for it is steadily increasing.

Of course Broadway and off Broadway, which is becoming just a less-expensive version of the big time, are still the goal and the fountainhead. After all, no one becomes a star simply because of an overwhelming success in Memphis. And no play in my memory has gone into theatre history direct from a production in Detroit. Nevertheless, all these new capital centers are just so many more steppingstones available to you.

Part Five: Today's Theatre

20. The Hits and the Flops

If you are one of that small group of benighted and inveterate latecomers at the theatre, you bustle in, breathless and apologetic, tramping on my feet no matter how far back under the seat I have them. I feel sorry for you, but I should also like to kick you, gently, as you pass. Especially I should like to kick you on opening nights when you crawl over the critics who have, of course, the aisle seats, and you spoil their mood.

I am well acquainted with these gentlemen; I was even married to one, a long time ago. I know that they come to an opening night actually longing to fall in love with the play, the musical, the star, or, best of all, an unknown whom they can make into a star that very night. They suffer as much as you do when they are trapped into having to judge a poor piece of work.

They are not responsible for a failure, as so many people claim. They do not gather in chatty groups to discuss the play's shortcomings, as is believed. They glumly stand alone or stay in their seats thinking up a good lead paragraph which will let you know—you who read nothing but first paragraphs and maybe the final one sometimes—their unhappy opinions.

Since there are only three major New York City daily newspapers, much is said and written about the tremendous power of the critics. But these men are not alone in their power to make or break. Just about the entire first-night audience consists of opinion-makers.

The "Hit" Play

If you are forgetful of the fact that openings start at seven or seven thirty and you arrive at intermission, you will know that the play is a hit by the beautiful, exciting hubbub all these beautiful and exciting people make. They are all as overjoyed as the authors, the actors, the producer, and the backers. The doorman, too, and especially the proprietor of the bistro next door, is overjoyed. It's a wonderful moment, even more thrilling than that dark one before the curtain rises.

That intermission happy buzz continues all through the run of a smash hit and it's heartwarming, even soul-satisfying, to watch the exodus when the final curtain falls, of gay, chattering, thoroughly satisfied theatre lovers.

The Slow Flop

On the other hand, the gloom around a failure covers everything in and near the theatre like a black frost.

Today, as we have seen, it is a question of a smash hit or a quick flop, unless there's that backlog of theatre parties which sometimes gives a production a million-dollar advance to sustain it. And so is born the slow flop. The theatregoers, having bought their tickets for some charitable purpose months in advance, feel obliged to attend even though they have read the notices and have been told just how boring and how bad an evening they will spend.

These are the theatre-party audiences that break actors' hearts. They seem to defy the people on the stage to entertain them. They refuse to laugh or applaud, and they look at each other almost guiltily, not only because they seem to feel stupid for having been entrapped, but also as though they were somehow to blame for it all. They drift out of the theatre and away while the show goes on.

The chairman of the event often goes around apologizing for her mistake in selecting this turkey. The actors usually prefer a quick death to such a painful, lingering one.

Why Flops?

But why do we have these million-dollar failures? Over and over again I am asked how it is that experienced and talented people end up with a product that absolutely no one likes. It is a mystery which is almost impossible to explain. It is really like trying to tell why a seemingly ideal marriage ends in divorce. Everything in the theatre starts with a love affair. But the theatrical affair involves many loves. The producer falls in love with a script, and the playwright immediately falls in love with the producer. Then a director is drawn into the love affair and after him come all the others—the set designer, the costume designer, the actors, even the hard-boiled press agent. Often they are all so blinded by love that they just cannot see that the object of all this outpouring is basically worthless.

And even a meritorious project can end in disaster, because there are so many things that can go wrong: miscasting, overproduction, technical mishaps, dull choreography, inappropriate or unattractive costumes and/or scenery, and unfortunate timing.

Timing is particularly important to success. Sometimes a production with what seems a fresh idea is in the works when another play or musical—even a television show or film—with the same basic premise arrives. I well remember how worried Lindsay and Crouse were about *Arsenic and Old Lace,* a comedy involving murder, when Alfred de Liagre also had in rehearsal *Mr. and Mrs. North,* another comedy about murder.

The jockeying of these two plays to be the first to open was intense: *Mr. and Mrs. North* was scheduled to open on a Tuesday and *Arsenic and Old Lace* the next night, Wednesday.

It was decided *Arsenic and Old Lace* would open on Monday, whereupon Mr. de Liagre switched his opening to Sunday. Mr. de Liagre thought he was safe because *Arsenic and Old Lace* was playing in Boston through Saturday. But it was so important to all concerned with *Arsenic and Old Lace* that they come in before *Mr. and Mrs. North* that they canceled the latter part of the week in Boston and opened in New York on Saturday. The play was a smash.

Mr. and Mrs. North received pleasant reviews, all comparing it with *Arsenic and Old Lace* in slightly patronizing terms. But it did have a nice long run anyway.

Who Makes the Success?

From the actor's viewpoint—the ambitious actor's—being in a smash hit which runs for two or three or more years is worse for his career than being in a dud in which he makes such a personal hit that he is immediately signed for another play or a television series or a film.

Some very good actors who stay with a hit show too long actually can be forgotten by producers and directors. Not the stars, of course; but few stars will sign for more than one season. Rex Harrison and Julie Andrews stayed in New York for less than one year of *My Fair Lady*'s six-year run; Zero Mostel was with *Fiddler on the Roof* only long enough to give it a good start; Walter Matthau and Art Carney were in *The Odd Couple* about a year and a half; Alan Arkin stayed in *Luv* nine months, leaving to make the film *The Russians Are Coming, The Russians Are Coming* which catapulted him to international stardom. But all left their marks—the imprint of their vivid personalities on the roles—which helped to give the production its original and triumphant mold.

Carol Channing played *Hello, Dolly!* only a year in New York and chose to tour with it in this country rather than to have the glamour of the London opening. Carol's astute and loving manager, her husband, had seen to it that she was paid a top percentage of the astronomical box-office receipts, and so, by the time Carol tired of Dolly Levi, she and Charles Lowe did not have to worry about any role to follow. Carol will always care, though, because she is a born trouper. She loves to perform and she has the same enthusiasm today that she had when I first saw her, skinny and huge-eyed, walk on stage in a cloche and a 1920s miniskirt to do the Gladiola Girl in the revue, *Lend an Ear*. It was in a tiny side-street theatre in Hollywood and I made a valiant effort to bring Carol and that charming show to Broadway, but I lost out to the Shuberts.

Nevertheless some stars do make a career of one part. Judith Anderson is the definitive *Medea*. She has been playing it since 1947. When I worked for the State Department at the Berlin Arts Festival in 1951 (the first time our government contributed money to a foreign cultural program), Judith's *Medea* was one of our showpieces. Another of our productions was *Oklahoma!* with Celeste Holm repeating her 1943 success as Ado Annie.

The fortunate stars—who are usually on a percentage basis of the box-office gross—manage to pile up substantial nest eggs and so do the fortunate producers, playwrights, and directors. But the big money that one hears about being made in the performing arts is seldom gained through the Broadway box office.

A thousand dollars a week has a glamorous, rich sound, and it is, indeed, a lot of money for an actor who is not one of the stars, but let us examine the thousand and see what it amounts to in the end. There are the withholding taxes which knock about $300 out of it to begin with. Then there is the agent's 10 percent which is another hundred. A personal press agent means another hundred, and, as one actor put it, "just living" takes at least three hundred dollars, so maybe two hundred dollars can be put aside toward "just living" during that long stretch which so often arrives between engagements.

It seems to me that the playwright today has the best chance of financial return, because good material is so scarce that a produced work, especially if it has some humor in it, is eagerly bid for by the television and film companies.

Producers and directors do the hardest work, and producers take the biggest gamble. Unless the play runs at least three weeks on or off-Broadway, the producer receives no part of any money that may accrue later although he may have worked a year, even two or more, to finance the play and make its New York birth possible.

The love affair I spoke of often remains intact, not only through all the trying days of preparation and rehearsal, but way, way beyond to solid success, and these partnerships, even amalgamations, are the bedrock of our enduring theatre.

A Final Word

I came to the theatre as a teen-age actress and I got my start—to answer that inevitable question—through my contacts —the very thing I have stressed as an important open sesame. Of course, after my first part, I too made the rounds.

I was one of the fortunate ones. Although my family at first was scandalized, since a theatre career was not an acceptable one for a young girl in those days, and they were convinced that they would be called upon to rescue me financially from such dire situations as being stranded in the Ozarks, I have managed to have an unspectacular but interesting and rewarding life and to make a decent living in and from the theatre. I was well educated, came from an intellectual family, and had learned a trade I could always have fallen back on. I was an expert in shorthand and typing, both of which I use to this day, before I ever stepped on a stage, and these skills gave me the fundamental confidence which is so necessary to every career. In fact, they were the bridge in my step from on stage to backstage.

When John Golden wanted to dictate a letter contract covering the play I had written with my acting partner, Dan Jarrett, he found to his annoyance that his secretary was at luncheon. I told him to dictate it to me and brought it back to him neatly typed in a few minutes.

It was the end of my acting career. I became part of Mr. Golden's production staff as script reviser with the playwright, casting director, costume and set supervisor, press agent, and general understudy for all feminine roles. It was wonderful training. I worked from ten in the morning until twelve at night and loved every minute of it.

Today a career in the theatre is highly regarded by even the most conservative families and, after the proper education and preparation, young talent is sent into the marketplace without too many fears and tears. But the road can still be rocky and usually is.

It takes an inner core of confidence and determination to suffer the outrageous fortune of those of us who labor in the theatre. But if you have the heart, the guts, and the talent—above all the talent—for it, the world of the performing arts is not only the most fascinating but the most rewarding place to be. Art endures. Its creators and co-workers are not forgotten. There is a special kind of immortality in having been part of it.

Part Six: Appendixes

Appendix 1.
Sample of a Résumé

(To be pasted on back of a photograph—or mailed without photograph to agents, directors, producers, etc.)

Name:	Jane Warner	Age Range: 18 to 23
Address:	600 West 55th St.	Height: 5′ 4″
	New York, N.Y. 10019	Weight: 118
Phone:	246–0000	Hair: Brown

BACKGROUND

Education: High School: Dennis-Yarmouth, South Yarmouth, Mass.
College: Emerson College, Boston, Mass. Theatre Arts Major
American Academy of Dramatic Arts, New York, N.Y.

ACTING EXPERIENCE

Off-Broadway:	Ivanov	Babakina
	Hobo (musical)	Judith
Touring:	Anniversary Waltz	Debbie
	Carnival	Lily
	The Matchmaker	Minnie Faye
	Ah! Wilderness	Muriel
Stock:	Take Her, She's Mine	Sarah
	Carnival	Princess Olga
	Bye Bye Birdie	Teenager
	Hamlet	Lady-in-Waiting
Television:	DuPont Show of the Week	
	Patty Duke	
	East Side—West Side	
Films:	Commercials	
	A Night in New York	
Additional Skills:	Dialects—French, Italian, Spanish	
	(Also knowledge of the languages)	
	Singing: Studied with ——	
	Dancing: " " "	

References:

Appendix 2.
Schools Offering Dramatic and
Musical Training

For colleges and courses on stage and backstage, write to

American Educational Theatre Association, Inc.
726 Jackson Place, N.W.
Washington, D.C. 20566
John F. Kennedy Center for the Performing Arts
Phone: (202) 343–8868, 8869

This organization publishes a paperback book called *The Directory of American College Theatre* which lists the regionally accredited two-year and four-year institutions in the fifty states and three Federally governed commonwealths. Over one thousand institutions are listed, giving not only the courses available in all phases of musical and dramatic theatre, but all technical courses, including lighting, scenic design, etc. It also lists all scholarships available.

The Directory of American College Theatre also lists all institutions in the country offering graduate study in the theatre with their courses and programs. Included, too, are tuition costs and financial aid assistance programs for students.

The book sells for $5.00 and can be secured from the association, but it may be found in virtually every public, university, and theatre library in the United States.

A special paperback, *You Can Win a Scholarship*, by Samuel C. Brownstein and Mitchel Weiner, is published by Barron's Educational Series, 113 Crossways Park Drive, Woodbury, N.Y. 11797. Third Revised Edition sells for $3.95.

It gives further detailed information on the steps to take to apply for a drama scholarship in virtually all of the one thousand universities listed in the American Educational Theatre Association directory. This book also may be found in just about every public, university, and theatre library in the country.

A scholarship opportunity for drama students already attending college is offered by the Radio Corporation of America, 30 Rockefeller Plaza, New York, N.Y. 10020. It is awarded to students majoring in dramatic arts and music.

The brochures and catalogues of almost all the schools listed below, alphabetically by state, list the scholarships and grants offered by the school.

California
Actors Studio, 1103 El Centro, Los Angeles, 90038.
Actors Theatre Workshop, 1058 N. Western Ave., Los Angeles, 90029.
Bard, Ben, 410 N. Beverly Drive, Beverly Hills, 90010.
Columbia College, 2328 West 7th St., Los Angeles, 90057.
Drama Workshop, 609 S. Westmoreland Ave., Los Angeles, 90005.
DuRoy, Bob, 744½ N. La Cienega Blvd., Los Angeles, 90069.
Falcon Studios, 5526 Hollywood Blvd., Hollywood, 90028.
Holloway, Elizabeth, 1638 Market St., San Francisco, 94102.
Krassner, Lela, 1346 N. La Brea Blvd., Hollywood, 90028.
Pasadena Playhouse, 39 S. El Molina Ave., Pasadena, 91101.
Professional Theatre Workshop, 780 Gower St., Hollywood, 90038.
Theatre-at-the-Schools, 4334 Van Nuys, Sherman Oaks, 91403.
Theatre of Arts, 5816 Wilshire Blvd., Los Angeles, 90036.
Three Arts Studio, 7233½ Santa Monica Blvd., Santa Monica, 90404.
Video Tape Workshop, 959 N. La Cienega Blvd., Los Angeles, 90069.

Colorado
Hacker Theatre School, 3268 Broadway, Denver, 80216.

Connecticut
Hartford Conservatory of Music, 834 Asylum Ave., Hartford, 06105.
Off-Broadway Talent, 306 Fairfield Ave., Bridgeport, 06603.

District of Columbia (Washington)
Valerie Warde School of Drama, 2753 Macomb, N.W., 20008.

Florida
Academy Royale Theatre, Inc., Royal Poinciana Playhouse, Palm Beach, 33480.
Guild Players Foundation, 4120 Herschel Ave., Jacksonville, 32210.
Merry-Go-Round Playhouse, 110 Aragon Ave., Coral Gables, 33134.
Studio M. Playhouse, 208 Bird Rd., Coral Gables, 33146.

Georgia
Academy Theatre, 3213 Roswell Rd., N.E., Atlanta, 30305.
Actors/Writers Workshop, 849 Juniper St., Atlanta, 30308.

Illinois
Harand Studios, 410 S. Michigan Ave., Chicago, 60605.
North Shore Academy/Theatre Arts, 1054 W. Wilson Ave., Chicago, 60640.
Theatre Art School, 5356 95th St., Oaklawn, 60453.

Iowa
Snook, Sylvia, 1122 6th Ave., Des Moines, 50314.

Kentucky
Carriage House, 1011 South 5th St., Louisville, 40203.

Louisiana
Mr. Lynn's School, 726 Cotton St., Shreveport, 71101.
Voss, Ruth, 2319 S. Carollton Ave., New Orleans, 70118.

Maine
Three Arts Studio, 115 High St., Portland, 04101.
Wilson, Sally, 263 State St., Portland, 04101.

Maryland
Bard-Avon School, Equitable Building, 8-12 N. Calvert St., Baltimore, 21202.

Massachusetts
Burchfield, Springfield Conservatory, 54 Byers St., Springfield, 01105.
Leland Powers School, 31 Evans Way, Boston, 02115.

Michigan
Detroit Institute of Musical Art, 5330 John Rd., Detroit, 48202.
Monte Carlo Studios, 10501 Puritan St., Detroit, 48238.

Minnesota
McPhail-Minneapolis School, 1128 La Salle Ave., Minneapolis, 55403.

Missouri
Anthony, Lenore, 3000 Campbell, Kansas City, 64109.

New Jersey

Sameret Performing Arts Center, Mount Freedom. Write to Florence Snyderman, 5900 Arlington Ave., Riverdale, N.Y. 10471.

Theatre Workshop, 646 Broadway, Newark, 07104.

New York

Actors Mobile Theatre, 2109 Broadway, New York, 10023.

Actors' Studio, 432 West 44th St., New York, 10036.

Adler, Frances, 30 West 72nd St., New York, 10023.

Stella Adler Theatre Studio, 1974 Broadway, New York, 10023.

American Academy of Dramatic Arts, 120 Madison Ave., New York, 10016.

American Center for Stanislavski Theatre Art, Inc., 485 Park Ave., New York, 10022.

American Musical and Dramatic Academy, 245 East 23rd St., New York, 10010.

American National Theatre & Academy (ANTA), for college students having had academic stage training, 245 West 52nd St., New York, 10019.

Dick Andros Theater Arts Center, 840 Flatbush Ave., Brooklyn, 11226.

Central Broadway Studios, 1647 Broadway, New York, 10019.

Circle in the Square Theatre School, 159 Bleecker St., New York, 10012.

Clark Center for Performing Arts, YWCA, 840 Eighth Ave., New York, 10019.

Comedia Puppet Players, 66 East 12th St., New York, 10003.

Directors Theatre School, 20 East 14th St., New York, 10003.

Ecole de Mime, 25 St. Marks Place, New York, 10003.

Gene Frankel Theatre Workshop, 115 MacDougal St., New York, 10012.

Gossett Academy of Dramatic Arts, 11 East 17th St., New York, 10003.

Group Theatre Workshop, 133 Second Ave., New York, 10003.

H. B. Studio, 120 Bank St., New York, 10014.

Institute for Advanced Studies in Theatre Art (IASTA), 418 West 42nd St., New York, 10036.

Juilliard School of Drama, Music School, Dance Division and the School of the American Ballet, Juilliard Building, Lincoln Center, New York, 10023. (1969.) Until open: International House, 500 Riverside Dr., New York, 10027.

Lewis, Robert, Claridge Hotel, Room 110, Broadway and 44th St., New York 10036.

Mackay, Suzanne (Suite 1210), 111 West 57th St., New York, 10019.

Art and Sonia Moore Studio of the Theatre, 485 Park Ave., New York, 10022.

Neighborhood Playhouse School, 340 East 54th St., New York, 10022.

New Theatre Workshop, 154 East 54th St., New York, 10022.

New York Academy of Theatrical Arts, 316 West 57th St., New York, 10019.

Pantomime Theatre of New York, 607 West End Ave., New York, 10024.

School of the Actors Company, 248 West 14th St., New York, 10011.

Senior Dramatic Workshop, 154 West 57th St., New York, 10019.

Max Slater Academy, 36 West 36th St., New York, 10018.

Stanleigh School of Theatre, 158 West 55th St., New York, 10019.

Studio Theatre School, 305 Lafayette Ave., Buffalo, 14213.

Theatre Laboratory, 1499 Northern Blvd., Roslyn, Long Island, 11576.

North Carolina

Masterson School, 501 Hemstead Place, Charlotte, 28207.

Ohio

Cincinnati Academy of Theatre, 3214 Woodburn Ave., Cincinnati, 45207.

Eyer, Walker, 28 East 6th St., Cincinnati, 45202.

Tolwig, Phyllis, 2440 Harrison Ave., Cincinnati, 45211.

Willson-Frazier School, 565 E. Town, Columbus, 43215.

Pennsylvania

Hedgerow Theatre School, Rose Valley Rd., Moylan, 19065.

Philadelphia Drama Workshop, 105 South 18th St., Philadelphia, 19103.

Pittsburgh Playhouse School of the Theatre, 222 Craft Ave., Pittsburgh, 15213.

Texas

Alley Theatre Academy, 709 Berry, Houston, 77002.

Black, Minerva, 4223 Southwest Freeway, Houston, 77027.

Churchill Way School, 6536 Churchill Way, Dallas, 75230.

Cocke School, 4031 University Blvd., Dallas, 75205.
Criner School, Bewley Building, 212 W. 7th St., Fort Worth,
76102.
Dallas Academy of Drama, 4419 Cole Ave., Dallas, 75205.
Dallas Theatre Centre, 3636 Turtle Creek Blvd., Dallas, 75219.
Theatre Three Academy, 2211 Main Street, Dallas, 75201.

Washington
Directors Studio, Fischer Studio Building, 1519 Third Ave., Seattle,
98101.

Wisconsin
Dixon, Jeanne, 7701 W. Fiebrantz Ave., Milwaukee, 53222.
Wisconsin Conservatory, 840 N. 3rd St., Milwaukee, 53203.
Wisconsin School of Music, 1584 N. Prospect Ave., Milwaukee,
53222.

Appendix 3.
Ballet and Dance Schools

A selection from the more than fourteen thousand dance schools in operation across America. For colleges and universities that teach serious dance, consult *Directory of Dance in Colleges and Universities* published by *Dance Magazine,* 268 West 47th St., New York, 10036. The schools listed below are devoted chiefly to ballet and/or modern dance, though many give instruction in tap, acrobatics, and ethnic dance forms.

Alabama
Birmingham Civic Ballet School, 2838 Highland Ave., Birmingham, 35205.

California
Academy of Ballet, 2121 Market St., San Francisco, 94114.
American School of Dance, 7021 Hollywood Blvd., Los Angeles, 90028.
St. Denis, Ruth, 3433 Cahuenga Blvd., West Hollywood, 90069.
San Diego Ballet, 3255 Fifth Ave., San Diego, 92103.
San Francisco Conservatory of Ballet, 925 O'Farrell St., San Francisco, 94109.
School of the San Francisco Ballet, 378 18th Ave., San Francisco, 94121.
Zoritch, George, 883 N. Westbourne, West Hollywood, 90069.

District of Columbia (Washington)
National Ballet School (School of National Ballet of Washington, with academic school, grades 11–12), 2801 Connecticut Ave., N.W., 20008.
Niketina-Sergieff, 5332 Sherrier Place, N.W., 20016.
Nirenska, Pola, 4601 Grant Rd., N.W., 20016.
Thimey, Erika, 2934 M St., N.W., 20007.
Washington School of the Ballet (with academic school, grades 11–12), 3515 Wisconsin Ave., N.W., 20016.

Florida
Imperial Studio/Ballet, Palm Beach Towers, Palm Beach, 33480.

Georgia
Atlanta School/Ballet, 3215 Cains Hills Place, N.W., Atlanta, 30305.

Illinois
Allegro American Ballet/School, 410 S. Michigan Ave., Chicago, 60605.
Keith Allison School of the Dance, 1902 Stevens Building, 17 N. State St., Chicago, 60602.
Ellis-Du Boulay School/Ballet, 20 E. Jackson, Chicago, 60604.
Stone-Camryn, 185 W. Madison, Chicago, 60602.

Massachusetts
Boston Conservatory of Music, 8 The Fenway, Boston, 02215.
Boston School of Ballet (E. Virginia Williams), 186 Massachusetts Ave., Boston, 02115.
Jacob's Pillow, Box 87, Lee, 01238.
Ana Joje School of Ballet, 669 Boylston St., Boston, 02130.

Michigan
Ricardeau, Enid, 28 W. Warren St., Detroit, 48201.
Severo School of Ballet, 5533 Woodward Ave., Detroit, 48202.

New Jersey
Firehouse Art Center, 187 Washington Ave., Coytesville, 07024.
Newark Ballet Academy, 11 Central Ave., Newark, 07102.
Newark Ballet Academy (Fred Danieli), 327 Main St., Newark, 07109.

New York
Ailey, Alvin, 25 West 65th St., New York, 10023.
American Academy of Dramatic Arts, 120 Madison Ave., New York, 10016.
American Ballet Center (School of City Center Joffrey Ballet), 434 Avenue of the Americas, New York, 10011.
American Ballet Theatre School (School of American Ballet Theatre), 316 West 57th St., New York, 10019.
American Musical and Dramatic Academy of New York, 245 East 23rd St., New York, 10010.
Dick Andros Theatre Arts Center, 840 Flatbush Ave., Brooklyn, 11226.
Anthony, Mary, 61 Fourth Ave., New York, 10003.
Ballet Arts School, 154 West 57th St., New York, 10019.
Ballet Repertory School, 200 East 56th St., New York, 10022.

Ballet Russe School, 24 West 57th St., New York, 10019.

Ballet Theatre School, 316 West 57th St., New York, 10019.

Bettis, Valerie, 34 East 10th St., New York, 10003.

Cunningham, Merce, 61 West 14th St., New York, 10011.

Dance Notation Bureau, 8 East 12th St., New York, 10003.

Eglevsky, Andre, 20 Unqua Road, Massapequa, Long Island, 11758.

Erdman, Jean, 110 West 14th St., New York, 10011.

Farnworth, Don, 1697 Broadway, New York, 10019.

Gelabert Studios, 257 West 86th St., New York, 10024.

Graham, Martha, 316 East 63rd St., New York, 10021.

Hadassah Dance/India, 45 Tieman Place, New York, 10027.

Harkness House/Ballet Arts, 4 East 75th St., New York, 10021.

Hawkins, Erik, 78 Fifth Ave., New York, 10003.

Henry Street Settlement Playhouse, 466 Grand St., New York, 10013.

Holm, Hanya, 1233 Avenue of the Americas, New York, 10019.

King, Bruce, 160 West 73rd St., New York, 10023.

Yurek Lazowski Academy, Wantagh, Long Island, 11793.

Luigi Jazz Center, 1721 Broadway, New York, 10019.

Metropolitan Opera Ballet School, Lincoln Center Plaza, New York, 10023.

Nagrin, Daniel, 21 Bleecker St., New York, 10012.

National Academy of Ballet (with academic school, grades 4–12), 200 East 56th St., New York, 10022.

Neighborhood Playhouse School of the Theatre, 340 East 54th St., New York, 10022.

New Dance Group, 254 West 47th St., New York, 10036.

Nossen, Steffi, 3 Winged Foot Drive, Larchmont, 10538.

Osgood-Morris Studio, 870 Broadway, New York, 10003.

Pandor, Miriam, 108 West 45th St., New York, 10036.

School of American Ballet, 2291 Broadway, New York, 10024.

Slavenska, Mia, 1233 Avenue of the Americas, New York, 10019.

Taylor, June, 1755 Broadway, New York, 10019.

Thomas-Fallis School of Ballet, 137 West 56th St., New York, 10023.

Truitte, James, 25 West 65th St., New York, 10023.

Weidman, Charles, 102 West 29th St., New York, 10001.

YM & YWHA, Lexington Ave. & 92nd St., New York, 10028.

Youskevitch, Igor, 846 Seventh Ave., New York, 10019.

Yuriko, 239 East 78th St., New York, 10021.

YWCA, Clark Center for the Performing Arts, 840 8th Ave., New York, 10019.

Ohio
Ballet Russe School, 3615 Euclid Ave., Cleveland, 44115.
Duncan, Marguerite, 822 Old Arcade, Cleveland, 44115.
Van Oettingen, Annaliese, 2461 Madison Rd., Cincinnati, 45208.

Oklahoma
Ranch Acres School of Ballet (Moscelyne Larkin and Roman Jasin-ski), 3315 East 33rd St., Tulsa, 74135.

Pennsylvania
Philadelphia Civic Ballet, 930 Chestnut St., Philadelphia, 19107.
Pittsburgh Playhouse School of the Theatre, 222 Craft Ave., Pittsburgh, 15213.
School of the Pennsylvania Ballet, 1924 Chestnut St., Philadelphia, 19103.

Texas
Etgen-Atkinson School of Ballet, 6815 Hillcrest, Dallas, 75205.
Houston Ballet Foundation (Nina Popova), 2018 W. Gray Ave., Houston, 77019.
Krassovska, Nathalie, 4228 Herschel, Dallas, 75219.

Tennessee
Ballet Society Academy, 2842 Poplar Ave., Memphis, 38111.

Utah
University of Utah Department of Dance (university offering a degree in dance, which also has a professional performing company, Utah Ballet), 1400 E. 2nd, S., Salt Lake City, 84112.

Washington
Nishitani, Martha, 4203 University Way, Seattle, 98105.

Appendix 4.
Voice Teachers and Coaches in New York City

Berghof, Herbert, 120 Bank St., 10014.
Bobrick, Gladys, 41 West 83rd St., 10024.
Burgess, June, 2109 Broadway, 10023.
Cooper, Edward, 1619 Broadway, 10019.
Frank, Claudia, 145 West 55th St., 10019.
Gorman, Robert, 140 West 58th St., 10019.
Greene, Allan, 1697 Broadway, 10019.
Hermes, Alice, 145 East 15th St., 10003.
Liebling, Estelle, 120 Central Park South, 10019.
Menotti, Carlo, 881 Seventh Ave., 10019.
Olson, J. Olaf, 43 West 93rd St., 10025.
Rich, Marian, 54 West 16th St., 10011.
Seton, Susan, 853 Seventh Ave., 10019.
Steele, Fred, 1650 Broadway, 10019.

Appendix 5.
Actors' Equity Theatre and Television Agents in New York City

(Area Code 212)

Actors and Authors Agency, 234 West 44th St., 10036. Phone: BR 9–7770.

Adler, Harry, 67 West 55th St., 10019. Phone: PL 7–2535. By appointment only.

Agency for the Performing Arts, 120 West 57th St., 10019. Phone: LT 1–8860.

Agneta, Nicholas, 1270 Avenue of the Americas, 10020. Phone: CO 5–0232. Productions, television, musicals, drama. Phone for an appointment.

Willard Alexander, Inc., 660 Madison Ave., 10021. Phone: PL 1–7070. General musical. Sees people Friday, 3 P.M. to 4 P.M. Band booking primarily.

All-Arts Talent Casting Agency, 850 Seventh Ave., 10019. Phone: JU 2–4933. General (all categories).

Almonte, Maria, 160 West 46th St., 10036. Phone: 246–7481. Thursday and Friday, 1 P.M to 6 P.M.

Anderson, Beverly, 117 West 48th St., 10036. Phone: 279–5553. Productions, stock, industrial shows, television, cinema, musicals, drama. Pictures and résumés. Will see only people whose work is known.

Arnold, Lillian, 119 West 57th St., 10019. Phone: PL 7–3400. Productions, television, dramatic. Write for appointment.

Artists Agency Corp., 1271 Avenue of the Americas, 10020. Phone: 765–5895. Send pictures and résumé.

Artists Management Associates, 200 West 57th St., 10019. Phone: PL 7–2157. General (all categories). Send picture and résumé.

Ashley Famous Artists, Inc., 1301 Avenue of the Americas, 10019. Phone: 965–5800. Send pictures and résumé.

Associated Booking Corp., 445 Park Ave., 10022. Phone: HA 1–5200. Sees people daily, 2:30 P.M to 6 P.M.

Astor, Richard, 119 West 57th St., 10019. Phone: LT 1–1970.

Barry Agency, The, 120 East 56th St., 10022. Phone: PL 1–0721.

Bonnie Kid Agency, 1674 Broadway, 10019. Phone: CI 6–0223. Television, juvenile. By appointment only, by phone. Children of all ages. Experience preferred.

Broder, Jane, 40 East 49th St., 10017. Phone: MU 8–0960. Sees people by appointment only.

Burk, Bernard, 48 West 48th St., 10036. Phone: PL 7–4540. Television, musicals. Sees people daily, 10:30 A.M. to 5 P.M.

Case, Bertha, 42 West 53rd St., 10019. Phone: LO 1–6280.

Cereghetti Agency, The, 156 West 44th St., 10036. Phone: 766–5260.

Cohen, Harold D., 600 Madison Ave., 10022. Phone: 935–4000.

Coleman, Raymond H., 30 West 60th St., 10023. Phone: CI 6–4232. Sees people by appointment only.

Coleman-Rosenberg Agency, 667 Madison Ave., 10021. Phone: TE 8–0734. Sees people by appointment only.

Bill Cooper Associates, 39 West 55th St., 10019. Phone: 265–4990. Sees people by appointment only.

Creative Management Association, 555 Madison Ave., 10022. Phone: MU 8–2020.

Deacy, Jane, 119 East 54th St., 10022. Phone: PL 2–4865. Sees people by appointment only.

Draper, Stephen, 37 West 57th St., 10019. Phone: HA 1–5780. Sees people by appointment only.

Eastman, Carl, 356 East 50th St., 10022. Phone: PL 1–5566. Television, dramatic. Sees people by appointment only.

Famous Artists, 44 West 44th St., 10036. Phone: CI 7–6200.

General Artists Corp., 600 Madison Ave., 10022. Phone: 935–4000. Productions, television, cinema, musical, dramatic. Sees people by appointment. Send photo and résumé, attention Mr. Sid Bernstein.

Gewald, Robert, 2 West 59th St., 10019. Phone: PL 3–0450. Television, general. Sees people by appointment only.

Goldsmith, George, 360 West 22nd St., 10011. Phone: CH 2–7060. Sees people by appointment only.

Janet Hall Artist Bureau, 111 West 57th St., 10019. Phone: CO 5–1673. Sees people by appointment only.

Hartig, Michael Frank, 105 West 55th St., 10019. Phone: PL 7–2224. Production, stock, industrial shows, television, cinema, musicals, dramatics. By appointment only.

Henry, Helen, 225 West 86th St., 10024. Phone: TR 7–4042. Phone for appointment only. Send pictures if appearing in a show.

Hesseltine, Bookman & Seff, Ltd., 157 West 57th St., 10019. Phone: LT 1–8850.

Hoffman, Hans J., 200 West 58th St., 10019. Phone: CI 6–1557. Production, musicals. Sees people by appointment only.

Hunt, Diana, 246 West 44th St., 10036. Phone: BR 9–0009. Production, television, cinema, musicals, dramatic. Phone for appointment, then send photos and résumé.

Hunter, Jeff, 119 West 57th St., 10019. Phone: 757–4995. Sees people by appointment only.

Irwin, Lou, 445 Park Ave., 10022. Phone: HA 1–5200.

International Talent Associates, 600 Madison Ave., 10022. Phone: 935–5995.

Jacobson, Leonard, 1650 Broadway, 10019. Phone: PL 7–3920. Television, musicals, dramatic. Sees people Tuesday, Wednesday, Thursday, 11 A.M. to 12 noon. Call for appointment first.

Joe Jordan Talent Agency, 400 Madison Ave., 10017. Phone: PL 5–2193.

Marvin Josephson Associates, Inc., 1271 Avenue of Americas, 10020. Phone: PL 7–8618.

Harriet Kaplan-Lily Veidt, Inc., 667 Madison Ave., 10021. Phone: PL 5–2214. Productions, television, cinema, industrial shows, musicals, dramatic. Sees people by appointment only.

Kennedy Artists, 400 Madison Ave., 10017. Phone: 675–3944. Sees people on Thursday. Call first. Accepts photos and résumés.

King, Archer, Room 3719, Time & Life Building, 10020. Phone: LT 1–8513. Phone for appointment only.

Kohler, Bob, 119 West 57th St., 10019. Phone: 765–1200. General, musicals, dramatic. Sees people by appointment only—phone first.

Tom Korman Associates, Inc., 225 West 57th St., 10019. Phone: LT 1–9040. Phone for appointment only.

Robert Lantz, Ltd., 111 West 57th St., 10019. Phone: PL 7–5076.

Leaverton Associates, Inc., 119 West 57th St., 10019. Phone: PL 7–4250. Sees people by appointment only.

Leaverton Associates, 850 Seventh Ave., 10019. Phone: LT 1–0907.

Leddy, Mark J., 225 West 57th St., 10019. Phone: JU 6–2760. Sees people by appointment only.

Lenny-Debin, 140 West 58th St., 10019. Phone: JU 2–0270. General. Sees people by appointment only. Pictures and résumés will be accepted by mail.

Leonard, Julie, 50 West 58th St., 10019. Phone: UN 5–1821. Productions, television, general. Sees people by appointment only.

Lester Lewis Associates, 15 East 48th St., 10017. Phone: PL 3–5083.

Liebling, William, 44 West 44th St., 10036. Phone: MU 7–5694. Productions, television, musicals, dramatic. Sees people by appointment only.

Dorothy Lohman Agency, 250 West 57th St., 10019. PL 7–1990.

William McCaffrey Agency, 501 Madison Ave., 10022. Phone: EL 5–1076. Television, general. Sees people by appointment only.

McClendon, Ernestine, 56 West 45th St., 10036. Phone: TN 7–2287. General.

Malone, Dudley Field, 330 West 45th St., 10036. Phone: 586–8255.

Meyer, Josh, 527 Madison Ave., 10022. Phone: PL 2–0515.

Miller, Dick, 1545 Broadway, 10036. Phone: LT 1–9161. Sees people by appointment only.

William Morris Agency, 1350 Avenue of the Americas, 10019. Phone: 586–5100. General. Sees people by appointment only.

Oscard, Fifi, 18 East 48th St., 10017. Phone: HA 1–4650. Sees people daily, 12:30 P.M to 3 P.M.

Ostertag, Barna, 501 Fifth Ave., 10017. Phone: OX 7–6339. Productions, dramatic. Sees people by appointment only.

People and Productions, Inc. (Marge Kerr), 333 East 55th St., 10022. Phone: 752–6436. By appointment only—phone.

Richard Pitman Agency, 229 West 42nd St., 10036. Phone: WI 7–5555. Sees people by appointment only.

Polan, Barron, 250 East 49th St., 10017. Phone: PL 9–4727. Productions, television, cinema, musicals, dramatic. Sees people by appointment only.

Richard, Max, 300 West 55th St., 10019. Phone: PL 7–6414. Productions, industrial, television, cinema, general.

Rivers, Tony, 154 West 54th St., 10019. Phone: PL 7–1185. Productions, cinema, dramatic. Sees people by appointment only.

Dick Rubin, Ltd., 200 West 57th St., 10019. Phone: 245–7810.

Ryan, Charles V., 35 West 53rd St., 10019. Phone: CI 5–2225. Industrial television, musicals. Sees people daily, 10 A.M. to 6 P.M.

Safier, Gloria, 667 Madison Ave., 10021. Phone: TE 8–4868. Productions, television, cinema, musicals, dramatic. Sees people by appointment only.

Sanford, Robert, 234 West 44th St., 10036. Phone: LO 3–4370. Cinema, general. By appointment only.

Schirmer, Gus, Jr., 147 East 62nd St., 10021. Phone: TE 8–3413. Productions, stock, industrial shows, cinema, general. By appointment only.

Schuller, William, 18 East 41st St., 10017. Phone: OR 9–5665. Photos and résumés received by mail only.

Shaw Artists Corp., 565 Fifth Ave., 10017. Phone: OX 7–7744. Variety, musicals. Sees people daily, 10 A.M. to 5 P.M.

Louis Shurr Agency, 1501 Broadway, 10036. Phone: CH 4–8240. Productions, television, general. Sees people daily, 10 A.M. to 12:30 P.M.

Silver, Monty, 850 Seventh Ave., 10019. Phone: 765–4040. Sees people Tuesday through Friday, 10 A.M. to 12 noon.

Soglio, Anthony, 423 Madison Ave., 10017. Phone: PL 9–3316. Productions, general. Call for appointment.

Stewart Artists Corp., 405 Park Ave., 10022. Phone: PL 2–0944.

Talent Representatives, 20 East 53rd St., 10022. Phone: PL 2–1835.

Michael Thomas Agency, 667 Madison Ave., 10021. Phone: 755–2616.

Tranum, Charles B., 603 Madison Ave., 10022. Phone: PL 1–3880. General. Sees people Monday, Wednesday, Friday, except 12 noon to 3 P.M.

United Talent, 157 West 57th St., 10019. Phone: 765-1200. Sees people by appointment only.

UTM Artists, Ltd., c/o GAC, 600 Madison Ave., 10022. Phone: 935–5988.

Webb-Cosden, 200 West 57th St., 10019. Phone: CO 5–4311. Productions, stock, industrial television, cinema, general. By appointment only. First mail pictures.

White, Mary Ellen, 415 Lexington Ave., 10017. Phone: 867–8350.

Wiese, Henry William, 1674 Broadway, 10019. Phone: CO 5–1930. Sees people Tuesday through Friday, 10 A.M. to 12 noon.

Peter Witt Associates, Inc., 37 West 57th St., 10019. Phone: PL 9–7966. Dramatic, productions, cinema. Sees people by appointment only.

Ann Wright Representatives, 850 Seventh Ave., 10019. Phone: CI 7–6470.

Appendix 6.
Play Agents in New York City

(Area Code 212)

American Play Company, 52 Vanderbilt Ave., 10017. Phone: MU 6–6333.
Brandt and Brandt, 101 Park Ave., 10017. Phone: MU 3–5890.
Burke, Shirley, 370 East 76th St., 10021. Phone: 861–2309.
Chambrun, Jacques, 745 Fifth Ave., 10022. Phone: PL 5–9464.
Curtis Brown, Ltd., 60 East 56th St., 10022. Phone: 755–4200.
Diamant, Anita, 51 East 42nd St., 10017. Phone: 687–1122.
Ann Elmo Agency, 545 Fifth Ave., 10017. Phone: MU 2–4327.
Fishbein, Frieda, 353 West 57th St., 10019. Phone: 247–4318.
Greenburger, Sanford, 595 Madison Ave., 10022. Phone: PL 3–8581.
Franz J. Horch Associates, 325 East 57th St., 10022. Phone: PL 3–9810.
Joseph, Nannine, 200 West 54th St., 10019. Phone: CI 7–4346.
Klausner, Bertha, 130 East 40th St., 10016. Phone: MU 5–2642, MU 3–9580.
Littauer & Wilkinson, 500 Fifth Ave., 10036. Phone: LW 4–3350.
McCall, Monica, 667 Madison Ave., 10021. Phone: TE 8–6650.
McIntosh & Otis, Inc., 18 East 41st St., 10017. Phone: MU 9–1050.
Richard Madden Play Co., 52 Vanderbilt Ave., 10017. Phone: MU 9–0354.
Matson, Harold, 22 East 40th St., 10016. Phone: 679–4490.
Meredith, Scott, 580 Fifth Ave., 10036. Phone: CI 5–5500.
Harold Ober Associates, 40 East 49th St., 10017. Phone: PL 9–8600.
Salisbury, Leah, 790 Madison Ave., 10021. Phone: 628–4404.
Schulberg, Mrs. Ad, 300 East 57th St., 10022. Phone: PL 9–1341.
Seligman, James F., 342 Madison Ave., 10017. Phone: YU 6–6013.
Wade Carlson Agency, 18 East 41st St., 10017. Phone: 683–1450.
Watkins, Ann, 77 Park Ave., 10016. Phone: LE 2–0080.
Williams, Annie Laurie, 18 East 41st St., 10017. Phone: MU 5–7564.

Writers Literary Agency, 40 West 72nd St., 10023. Phone: TR 3–2185, EN 2–6100.

Writers Workshop, Inc., 51 East 42nd St., 10017. Phone: 687–1122.

Appendix 7.
Active Producers in New York City

Abbott, Michael, 235 West 47th St., 10036.
Balding, Ivor David, 154 East 54th St., 10022.
Black, David, 1501 Broadway, 10036.
Bloomgarden, Kermit, 1545 Broadway, 10036.
Brisson, Frederick, 745 Fifth Ave., 10022.
Cates, Gilbert, 101 West 57th St., 10019.
Cates, Joseph, and Henry Fownes, 120 East 56th St., 10022.
Coe, Fred, 718 Madison Ave., 10021.
Cohen, Alexander H., 225 West 44th St., 10036.
Crawford, Cheryl, & Richard Chandler, 165 West 46th St., 10036.
Dalrymple, Jean, 130 West 56th St., 10019.
de Liagre, Alfred, Jr., 55 West 42nd St., 10036.
Elkins, Hillard, 19½ East 62nd St., 10021.
Ellis, Michael, 850 Seventh Ave., 10019.
Erskine, Howard, & Joseph Hayes, 18 West 55th St., 10019.
Feuer, Cy, & Ernest H. Martin, 505 Park Ave., 10022.
Fryer, Carr & Harris, 445 Park Ave., 10022.
Gordon, Stanley, 850 Seventh Ave., 10019.
Gottlieb, Morton, & Helen Bonfils, 1564 Broadway, 10036.
Hayward, Leland, 655 Madison Ave., 10021
Hollywood, Daniel, & Seymour Vall, 130 West 57th St., 10019.
Kanin, Garson, 1650 Broadway, 10019.
Kanin, Michael, 62 West 45th St., 10036.
Lansbury, Edgar, 888 Eighth Ave., 10019.
Lester, Edwin, Curran Theater, 445 Geary St., San Francisco, Calif.,
    94102, & Lawrence Shubert Lawrence, 236 West 44th St.,
    10036.
Levin, Herman, 424 Madison Ave., 10017.
Liebman, Max, & Albert Lewis, 165 West 46th St., 10036.
Mann, Theodore, Circle in the Square, 159 Bleecker St., 10012.
Martin, Elliot, 101 West 57th St., 10019.
Merrick, David, 246 West 44th St., 10036.
Gilbert Miller Productions, Henry Miller's Theatre, 124 West 43rd
    St., 10036.
Miller, Mitch, 345 West 58th St., 10019.

Osterman, Lester, 1650 Broadway, 10019.
Ostrow, Stuart, 1501 Broadway, 10036.
Peck, Charles K., Jr., & Frederico Fellini, 165 West 46th St., 10036.
Perry, Elaine, & Charles Hollerith, Jr., 137 West 48th St., 10036.
Phoenix-APA Repertory Co., 149 West 45th St., 10036.
Preminger, Otto, 711 Fifth Ave., 10022.
Prince, Harold, 1 Rockefeller Plaza, 10020.
Producers Managers Co., 330 West 45th St., 10036.
Quartet Productions, 234 West 44th St., 10036.
Ramin, Jordan, & Charles Reinhart, 150 West 52nd St., 10019.
Repertory Theater of Lincoln Center, Lincoln Center Plaza, 10023.
Rodgers, Richard, 598 Madison Ave., 10022.
Roy, Susan, 1564 Broadway, 10036.
Subber, Saint, 116 East 64th St., 10021.
Saxon, Don, 400 East 52nd St., 10022.
Schary, Dore, 850 Seventh Ave., 10019.
Selden, Albert, 119 West 57th St., 10019.
Sharmat, Stephen W., 234 West 44th St., 10036.
Sheldon, David, 135 West 58th St., 10019.
Showtime Productions, 55 West 42nd St., 10036.
Shull, Leo, 136 West 44th St., 10036.
Silverman, Hy (Helicon Productions), 306 West 73rd St., 10023.
Stoddard, Haila, 435 West 57th St., 10019.
Tamarack Theatre, 1564 Broadway, 10036.
Temma Productions, 1674 Broadway, 10019.
Theatre Guild, 226 West 47th St., 10036.
Whitehead, Robert, 1545 Broadway, 10036.
Whitelaw, Arthur, & Frank Bessell, 34 West 10th St., 10011.
Willey, Robert, 152 West 42nd St., 10036.
York, Richard, 17 West 71st St., 10023.

Appendix 8.
Off-Broadway Theatres and Producers

Theatres and Their Producers (Area Code 212)

American Place Theatre, 423 West 46th St., 10036. Phone: 246–3730.

Astor Place Theatre, 434 Lafayette St., 10003. Phone: AL 4–4060. *Producer:* Ruth Newton, Diane Mathews.

Bert Wheeler Theatre, 250 West 43rd St., 10036. Phone: JU 6–7954. *Producer:* Curley Company.

Bil Baird Theatre, 59 Barrow St., 10014. Phone: LO 3–4370. *Producer:* Arthur Cantor.

Cherry Lane Theatre, 38 Commerce St., 10014. Phone: YU 9–2020. *Manager:* Joseph Beruh.

Circle in the Square, 159 Bleecker St., 10012. Phone: AL 4–2150. *Producer:* Theodore Mann.

Forum Theatre, Broadway & 47th St., 10036. Phone: EN 2–7600. *Producer:* Lincoln Center Repertory.

Jan Hus Theatre, 351 East 74th St., 10021. Phone: LE 5–6310. *Producer:* Jack Irving.

Judson Poets' Theatre, Judson Memorial Church, 55 Washington Square South, 10012. Phone: SP 7–0033. *Producer:* Al Carmines.

Martinique Theatre, 32nd St. & Broadway, 10001. Phone: 246–3730. *Producer:* American Place Theatre Group.

Negro Ensemble Co., 1545 Broadway, 10036. Phone: JU 2–5250.

New Theatre, 154 East 54th St., 10022. Phone: PL 2–1370. *Producers:* I. D. Balding, A. Ferleger, G. Crowe.

Orpheum Theatre, 126 Second Ave., 10003. Phone: 246–8488. *Producers:* Zev Bufman, Dorothy Love.

Players Theatre, 115 MacDougal St., 10012. Phone: AL 4–5076. *Producer:* Monroe Productions.

Pocket Theatre, 100 Third Ave., 10003. Phone: YU 2–0155. *Producer:* Stephanie Sills.

Public Theatre, 425 Lafayette St., 10003. Phone: 677–3750. *Producer:* New York Shakespeare Festival. *Director:* Joseph Papp.

St. Marks Playhouse, 133 Second Ave., 10003. Phone: 765–9727. *Producers:* Arthur Whitelaw, Gene Persson.

Sheridan Square Playhouse, 99 Seventh Ave., 10011. Phone: CH 2–3432. *Producer:* Dwubba Productions.

Stage Theatre, 321 East 73rd St., 10021. Phone: BU 8–2500. *Producers:* William Dorr, Michael White.

Sullivan Street Playhouse, 181 Sullivan St., 10012. Phone: JU 6–3433. *Producers:* Lore Noto, S. Baron, Dorothy Olim.

Theatre De Lys, 121 Christopher St., 10014. Phone: WA 4–8782. *Producer:* Paul B. Berkowsky.

Theatre Four, 424 West 55th St., 10019. Phone: 246–8545. *Producer:* Richard Barr.

Village Gate, Bleecker & Thompson Sts., 10012. Phone: CI 5–8553. *Producer:* 3W Productions.

Major Off-Broadway Managers

Berkowsky, Paul B., Theatre De Lys, 121 Christopher St., 10014.

Beruh, Joe, Suite 7-C, 888 Eighth Ave., 10019.

Krone-Olim Management, 1545 Broadway, 10036. *General Manager:* Erin Clermont, Assoc.

Libin, Paul, Martinique Theatre, 32nd St. & Broadway, 10001.

Turner, Lily, 62 Perry St., 10014.

Appendix 9.
Off-Off-Broadway Theatres and Producers

Afro-American Folkloric Troupe, 13th Street Theatre, 50 West 13th
St., 10011. *Producer:* Bro Herrod.

Anthony Mannino Repertory Club, 182 Fifth Ave. (at) 23rd St.,
10010. *Producer:* Scott Kalman.

Channel 1, Underground Television, 62 East 4th St., 10003. *Producer:* Kenneth Shapiro.

Columbia University Teachers College Drama Workshop, Broadway & 120th St., 10027. *Producers:* Dr. Paul Kozelka or Dr.
Gilbert N. Lazier.

Dove Company, St. Peter's Church, 346 West 20th St., 10011.
Director: Harold Herbstman.

Downstage Studio Theatre, 321 West 14th St., 10014. *Producer:*
Charles Stewart.

Dramarena, 158 West 55th St., 10019. *Producers:* Pauline Braun
and David Sawn.

Dramatic Workshop, Carnegie Hall Building, 881 Seventh Ave.,
10019. *Director-Producer:* Victor Glover.

Gene Frankel Repertory Theatre, 115 MacDougal St., 10012. *Producer:* Gene Frankel.

Hayes Theatre Workshop, 1741 Broadway, 10019. *Producer:* Vickie
Hayes.

Hilly's, 62 West 9th St., 10011. *Producer:* Hilly Kristal.

John Jay College of Criminal Justice, 235 East 20th St., 10003.
The Dramateurs. *Producer:* Professor Ben Termine.

Lincoln Center Repertory Co., Lincoln Center Plaza, 10023. *Producer:* Jules Irving.

Master Theatre, 103rd St. & Riverside Dr., 10025. *Producer:* Equity
Theatre. *Managing Director:* George Wojtasik.

Playbox, 94 St. Marks Place, 10009. *Producer:* Robert Weinstein.

Courtyard Playhouse, 424 West 45th St., 10036. *Producer:* Bob
Stark.

Playwrights Work Shop Club, Inc., Bastiano's Cellar Studio, 14
Waverly Place, 10003. *Producer:* N'Thoni Bastiano.

Royal Playhouse, 219 Second Ave., 10003. *Producer:* Rose Lynch.

Roundabout Theatre, 307 West 26th St., 10001. *Producer:* Gene Feist.

Rutgers Church, C.S.C. Repertory Theatre, 236 West 73rd St., 10023. *Producer:* Christopher Martin.

Senior Dramatic Workshop, Carnegie Hall, 831 Seventh Ave., 10019. *Producer:* Victor Glover.

Tambellini's Gate Theatre, Second Ave. & 10th St., 10019. *Director:* Charles Ludlam.

13th Street Theatre, 50 West 13th St., 10011. *Producers:* Jacob Millstein and Jordon Hott, 285 Riverside Dr., 10025.

Troupe Theatre, 167 West 21st St., 10011. *Producer:* Christopher St. John.

Village Gate, Bleecker and Thompson Sts., 10012. 3 W Productions. *Producer:* Eric Blau.

Appendix 10.
Repertory Theatres
(Nonprofit Professional Theatres)

Theatre Communications Group (TCG), 20 West 43rd St., New York, 10036, Phone: LO 3–0072, is a nonprofit organization founded in 1961 designed to help strengthen the standards of resident professional theatres, repertory theatres, and university theatres in America. It is concerned with professional theatres established throughout the country as nonprofit organizations, devoted to employing resident companies to perform serious drama. TCG theatres are listed by state. Write to the TCG office in New York for specific inquiries.

California
American Conservatory Theatre, Geary Theatre, 450 Geary St., San Francisco, 94102.
Center Theatre Group, 135 N. Grand Ave., Los Angeles, 90012.
Huntington Hartford Theatre, 1615 Vine St., Los Angeles, 90028.
Stanford Repertory Theatre, Memorial Auditorium, Stanford University, Stanford, 94305.

Connecticut
Hartford Stage Co., 65 Kinsley St., Hartford, 06103.
Long Wharf Theatre, Frontage Rd., New Haven, 06511.

Delaware
Playhouse, DuPont Building, Wilmington, 19801.

District of Columbia (Washington)
National Theatre, 1321 E St., 20004.

Illinois
Studebaker Theatre, 418 S. Michigan Ave., Chicago, 60605.

Kentucky
Actors Theatre of Louisville, North 7th St., Louisville, 40202.
Brown Theatre, 315 W. Broadway, Louisville, 40202.

Louisiana
Civic Theatre, 533 Baronne St., New Orleans, 70113.
Repertory Theatre of New Orleans, 546 Carondelet, New Orleans, 70130.

Maryland
Center Stage, 11 E. North Ave., Baltimore, 21202.

Massachusetts
Theatre Company of Boston, 200 Tremont St., Boston, 02111.
Charles Playhouse, 76 Warrenton St., Boston, 02116.

Michigan
Association of Producing Artists, Central Campus, University of Michigan, Ann Arbor, 48104.

Minnesota
Minnesota Theatre Co., Tyrone Guthrie Theatre, 725 Vineland Place, Minneapolis, 55403.

Missouri
American Theatre, 9th and St. Charles Sts., St. Louis, 63101.

New York
Association of Producing Artists, Lyceum Theatre, 149 West 45th St., New York, 10036.
National Repertory Theatre, 360 East 55th St., New York, 10022.
Repertory Theatre of Lincoln Center, The, 150 West 65th St., New York, 10023.
Studio Arena Theatre, 681 Main St., Buffalo, 14203.

North Carolina
Aycock Auditorium, University of North Carolina, Greensboro, 27412.

Ohio
Cleveland Play House, 2040 East 86th St., Cleveland, 44106.
Hanna Theatre, 640 Hanna Building, Cleveland, 44115.
Hartman Theatre, 79 E. State St., Columbus, 43215.
Shubert Theatre, 701 Walnut St., Cincinnati, 45202.

Oklahoma
Mummers Theatre, 1108 W. Main St., Oklahoma City, 73106.

Pennsylvania
Theatre of the Living Arts, 334 South St., Philadelphia, 19147.
William Goldman Theatre, 15th and Chestnut Sts., Philadelphia, 19102.

Rhode Island
Trinity Square Repertory Co., Trinity Square Playhouse, 7 Bridgham St., Providence, 02907.

Tennessee
Front Street Theatre, 1819 Madison Ave., Memphis, 38104.

Texas
Alley Theatre, 709 Berry Ave., Houston, 77002.

Virginia
Barter Theatre, Abingdon, 24210.

Washington
Seattle Repertory Theatre, Seattle Center, P. O. Box B, Queen Anne Station, Seattle, 98109.

Wisconsin
Milwaukee Repertory Theatre, 2842 N. Oakland Ave., Milwaukee, 53211.

Appendix 11.
Summer Stock Theatres

Colorado

Elitch Theatre Co., 4620 West 38 Ave., Denver, 80212. Phone: (303) 455–4771.
Producer-Manager: Whitfield Connor, 435 West 57th St., New York, 10019. Phone: (212) 245–3455.

Connecticut

Candlewood Playhouse, New Fairfield, 06810.
Producer-Manager: Alton Wilkes, 152 Blueberry Lane, Laconia, N.H. 03246. Until June: Wellington Hotel, Seventh Ave. & 55th St., New York, 10019. Phone: (212) CI 7–3900.
Ivoryton Playhouse, Ivoryton, 06442. Phone: (203) SO 7–8258.
Producer-Manager: Milton Stiefel, Wellington Hotel, Seventh Ave. & 55th St., New York, 10019. Phone: (212) 765–4094.
Westport Country Playhouse, Westport, 06880. Phone: (203) 227–5138. New York tie line: (212) CI 6–1614.
Producers-Managers: James B. McKenzie, Spofford Beadle, Ralph Roseman, Producing Managers Co., 330 West 45th St., New York, 10036. Phone: (212) LT 1–2620.

Florida

Cocoanut Grove Playhouse, 3500 Main Highway, Miami, 33133.
General-Manager: Norman Rothstein.
Producer-Manager: Zev Bufman, 330 West 45th St., New York, 10036. Phone: (212) 246–8488.
Parker Playhouse, Box 4603, Fort Lauderdale, 33304.
Producer-Manager: Zev Bufman, 330 West 45th St., New York, 10036. Phone: (212) 246–8488.
Royal Poinciana Playhouse, Box 231, Palm Beach, 33480. Phone: (305) TE 3–8543.
Producers-Managers: Frank Hale, James B. McKenzie, 330 West 45th St., New York, 10036. Phone: (212) LT 1–2620.

Illinois

Little Theatre on the Square, Sullivan, 61951.
Producer-Manager: Guy S. Little, Jr. Phone: (217) 728–8522.

Maine
Kennebunkport Playhouse, Kennebunkport, 04046. Phone: (207) 967–3329.
> *Producer-Manager:* Mye Eolis, 17 West 71st St., New York, 10023. Phone: (212) 799–6480.

Lakewood Theatre, Skowhegan, 04976. Phone: (207) GR 4–3331.
> *Producer-Manager:* Henry Richards, 200 East 36th St., New York, 10016. Phone: (212) OR 9–4962.

Ogunquit Playhouse, Ogunquit, 03907. Phone: (207) 646–5511, (207) 646–3307.
> *Producer-Manager:* John Lane, 136 East 55th St., New York, 10022. Phone: (212) PL 1–5363.

Massachusetts
Falmouth Playhouse, Coonamessett. Phone: (617) LO 3–6622.
> *Producer-Manager:* Sidney Gordon, 25 Sutton Place, New York, 10022. Phone: (212) PL 3–1330.

Lake Whalom Playhouse, Fitchburg, 01420. Phone: (617) DI 5–4334.
> *Producer-Manager:* Guy Palmerton, 215 West 55th St., 10019. Phone: (212) CI 6–2280, (212) CI 7–2000.

New Hampshire
Lakes Region Playhouse, Laconia, Glendale, 03246. Phone: (603) CY 3–4387.
> *Producer-Manager:* Alton Wilkes, 152 Blueberry Lane, Laconia, N.H. 03246. Until June: Wellington Hotel, Seventh Ave. & 55th St., New York, 10019. Phone: (212) CI 7–3900.

New Jersey
Paper Mill Playhouse, Millburn, 07041. Phone: (201) DR 9–3636. New York tie line: (212) WH 4–4955.
> *Producer-Manager:* Frank Carrington, 330 West 45th St., New York 10036. Phone: (212) CO 5–3995.

Playhouse-on-the-Mall, Bergen Mall, Paramus, 07652. Phone: (201) HU 9–2030.
> *Producer-Manager:* Robert Ludlum, Bergen Mall, Paramus, 07652. Phone: (201) HU 9–3938.

New York
Colonie Summer Theatre, Latham, 12110. Phone: (518) 785–0880.

Producer-Manager: Eddie Rich, 340 East 64th St., New York, 10021. Phone: (212) HA 1–9255.

Corning Summer Theatre, Box 51, Corning, 14830. Phone: (607) 936–4634.

Producer-Manager: Dorothy Chernuck, 220 East 52nd St., New York, 10022. Phone: (212) PL 2–8437.

John Drew Theatre, East Hampton, L.I., 11937. Phone: (516) 324–0806.

Producer-Manager: Conrad Thibault, Ansonia Hotel, 73rd St. & Broadway, New York, 10023. Phone: (212) 362–0035.

Mineola Theatre, Mineola, L.I., 11501. Phone: (516) CH 8–5620.

Producer-Manager: Robert Fishko, Box 711, Mineola, L.I., 11501. Phone: (212) AX 1–5550.

Tappan Zee Playhouse, Nyack, 10960. Phone: (914) EL 8–5800.

Producer-Manager: Bruce Becker, 575 Madison Ave., New York, 10022. Phone: (212) PL 2–5535.

Pennsylvania

Bucks County Playhouse, New Hope, 18938. Phone: (215) 862–2046.

Producer-Manager: Walter Perner, Jr., 850 Seventh Ave., New York, 10019. Phone: (212) JU 2–4960.

Music Fairs Enterprises, Playhouse-in-the-Park, West Fairmount Park, Philadelphia, 19131. Phone: (215) MA 7–1300, (215) GR 7–1122.

Producers-Managers: Marvin Krauss, Jeremy Ritzer, Music Fairs, Inc., 40 West 55th St., New York, 10019. Phone: (212) LT 1–3250.

Pocono Playhouse, Mountainhome, 18342. Phone: (717) 595–7456.

Producer-Manager: Rowena Stevens, 15 East 48th St., New York, 10017. Phone: (212) PL 8–1520, (212) PL 5–9383.

For a complete list of summer theatres in the United States, consult the booklet entitled *Summer Theatre,* published every year in the early spring, on sale at any of the newsstands in the New York theatre district. You can get it by writing: *Show Business,* 136 West 44th St., New York, 10036.

Appendix 12.
Dinner Theatres

[E] indicates Equity

After-Dinner Productions, 50 West 67th St., New York, N.Y. 10023. *Producer:* Mervin Nelson. Theatre in Richmond, Va. [E].

American Players, Suite 332, 527 Lexington Ave., New York, N.Y. 10017. *Producer:* James Woodward. Theatres in Chattanooga, Kingsport, Memphis, Tenn.; Little Rock, Ark.

Atlanta Dinner Theatre, 2939 Campbellton Road, S.W., Atlanta, Ga. 30311 [E].

Lancer Productions, 158 West 55th St., New York, N.Y. 10023. *Managing Director:* Arlen Digitale.

Meadowbrook Dinner Theatre, Cedar Grove, N.J., 07009 [E].

Oregon Ridge Dinner Theatre, P. O. Box 95, Cockeysville, Md. 21030. *Manager:* Charles H. Dorsey, Jr.

Theatre Productions, 1697 Broadway, New York, N.Y. 10019. *Producer:* Howard Wolfe. Theatres in Richmond and Roanoke, Va.; Greensboro, Raleigh, Charlotte, N.C.; Knoxville, Nashville, Tenn.; Dallas, Tex. [E] and [Non-E].

Wedgewood Dinner Theatre, 1016 Cedar Swamp Rd., Glen Cove, Long Island, N.Y. 11542. *Producer:* Paul C. Iddings [E].

Appendix 13.

Minimum Weekly Salary for Actors' Equity Performers and Backstage Workers

(As of June 1, 1968)

ACTORS: DRAMATIC AND MUSICAL

Broadway

1968	$145.00	Plus	cost-of-living	increase
1969	150.00	"	"	"
1970	155.00	"	"	"

Road

1968	$195.00	"	"	"
1969	200.00	"	"	"
1970	205.00	"	"	"

Resident and Repertory Theatres

1968	Principals	$142.50	1969	$150.00
"	Actors	125.00	"	130.00
"	Chorus	107.50	"	115.00
"	Extras	90.00	"	95.00

Resident Stock Dramatic and Musical
1968 (Company whose potential gross is $13,500 per week or
    more)
    Actors $120.00
    (More than $7,500 but less than $13,500 gross)
    Actors   110.00
    (Less than $7,500 per week gross)
    Actors   90.00

Nonresident Stock Dramatic
1968 Actors $115.00

Nonresident Stock Musical
1968 Actors $115.00

Off-Broadway Dramatic and Musical

Weekly Box Office Gross	Actors Minimum		
	1968	*1969*	*1970*
Under $4,500	$ 70.00	$ 72.50	$ 75.00
Over $4,500–5,500	75.00	77.50	80.00
Over 5,500–6,500	85.00	87.50	90.00
Over 6,500–7,500	95.00	97.50	100.00
Over 8,500–9,500	130.00	132.50	135.00
Over 9,500	145.00	147.50	150.00

STAGE MANAGERS

Dramatic Broadway
1968	$242.45	Plus	cost-of-living	increase
1969	247.45	"	"	"
1970	252.45	"	"	"

Dramatic Road
1968	292.45	"	"	"
1969	297.45	"	"	"
1970	302.45	"	"	"

Musical Broadway
1968	293.05	"	"	"
1969	298.05	"	"	"
1970	303.05	"	"	"

Musical Road
1968	343.05	"	"	"
1969	348.05	"	"	"
1970	353.05	"	"	"

1st Assistant Stage Manager

Dramatic Broadway
1968	$181.70	Plus	cost-of-living-increase
1969	186.70	"	"	"
1970	191.70	"	"	"

Dramatic Road
1968	231.70	"	"	"
1969	236.70	"	"	"
1970	241.70	"	"	"

STAGE MANAGERS (*cont'd*)

Musical Broadway
    1968   212.10   "   "   "
    1969   217.10   "   "   "
    1970   222.10   "   "   "

Musical Road
    1968   262.10   "   "   "
    1969   267.10   "   "   "
    1970   272.10   "   "   "

Resident and Repertory (Based on weekly gross receipts)

1968	Minimum	"A"	$24,000	and over	$260.00	1969:	$275.00
"	"	"B"	12,000	to 24,000	200.00	"	205.00
"	"	"C"	6,000	to 12,000	160.00	"	165.00
"	"	"D"	Up	to $6,000	140.00	"	150.00

Resident Dramatic Stock
    Minimum Contract for stock: 1968—$110.00 per week

Nonresident Dramatic Stock
    1968 $160.00 per week

Musical Stock
    1968 $170.00 per week

Off-Broadway
    Stage managers' minimum salary shall be $20.00 higher than the applicable minimum salary for actors.
    Assistant stage managers' minimum salary shall be at least $10.00 higher than the applicable minimum salary for actors.

Index

Index

(Italicized numbers indicate illustrations)

250   Index